How to Get Published Free

D0619564

How to Get Published Free
Best in
Self-
Publishing
& Print on Demand

Plus Marketing Your
Book on The Internet

by
David Rising

Third Edition

Published by
Reality Publishing ink
Morganton, N.C. 28655

ISBN 978-1-4116-6001-4

Library of Congress Control Number: 2005902977

This book can be purchased at:
Realitypublishingink.com

The author can be contacted at:
David@realitypublishingink.com

Table of Contents

Disclaimer

This book is meant to be a general manual to help you understand the self-publishing and the print on demand process. It isn't the definitive answer to writing and publishing.

The author doesn't claim to guarantee you, the reader, instant success from reading this material. Any success you attain will be determined by your willingness to work diligently and to learn as much as you can about the subject matter that you'll be writing about.

The author doesn't claim to offer legal or other professional advice in this book. If you need professional services, you should seek a professional expert in the field of your need.

A good portion of the information in this book is designed based on how several websites conduct business. Their information or the way they conduct day to day business could change in an instant, which could result with some material in this book becoming obsolete. To the best of my knowledge all information in this book was current on the published date.

Some websites, especially Amazon, are always tweaking their sites to make improvements. If and when a certain amount of the information in this book becomes outdated and obsolete, I'll make an honest effort to update the material by publishing a new edition.

The author shall not be held liable for any financial losses allegedly resulting from the information in this book.

Introduction

Occasionally something will happen in a particular industry that creates a level playing field for all participates. It's definitely a rare occurrence, but it does happen. This usually happens when something new has been introduced to an old established industry, or it could be that someone came up with a better way of doing something that has been around forever. In a of lot instances an old established company will refuse to try anything new if the way they have been doing business is still paying the bills. So, it usually falls on the newer and more dynamic companies that are willing to take chances and introduce new trends that shake up the old way of doing business. If this new approach of doing an old business turns out to be a great idea and most participants and customers take to it, then the new dynamic company could feasibly wind up leaving the old companies in the dust and wondering what happened.

Well, this is the case in the publishing industry. New technologies have been introduced to the publishing industry in the last few years and the young dynamic companies are honing the tools to perfection. While the traditional publishing houses have continued to do business as usual, new **Print on Demand** publishing companies have arrived on the scene.

This new breed is unlike the traditional publishers that will only accept maybe two or three percent of manuscripts submitted and reject the rest. There are tons of well-respected authors that had to go through this grueling process before finally being accepted by a traditional publisher. If you have submitted your manuscript to agents and publishers just to receive a rejection slip several months later don't worry, you won't get a rejection slip here.

Introduction

We are entering into a new age of publishing. Like the Xerox commercial points out, everyone can now be published. With new Print on Demand (POD) technologies, the savvy author can now self-publish without paying thousands of dollars to have a batch of books printed up in advance. Print on Demand publishing means exactly what it implies, books are only printed when ordered. This publishing method is also environmentally friendly. There isn't going to be thousands of unsold books to be disposed of. The author can bypass the vanity press route that required batches of books to be printed in advance. There is no longer a need to wait six months or more for a rejection letter from a traditional publishing house or agent. The author's destiny is now absolutely in his or her hands.

There is at least one young dynamic Print on Demand publishing company that is welcoming all comers to join the new publishing revolution. It doesn't matter if you're a seasoned writer or a beginning novice there's a spot for you. If you the author can produce a top notch, error free and interesting manuscript, you will stand as good of a chance in succeeding as the next person. Basically what I'm saying is that it is now much easier to get published, but to be successful, as in any venture, it will still require hard work and dedication. You might not have much money to invest in your writing, but you can compensate with extraordinary resolve.

What to Publish

So, how do you get started at getting something published? The question is to be or not to be a writer. The common problem beginners have, is they think they must produce a full-scale novel from the starting gates. There are many ways and many products that can be published. Start small at first, get your feet wet, unless you just have to do that novel first, then go for it. But you should consider looking at material that doesn't require as much work to begin with.

There's a story or two in everyone, it's your life and you may think it has been a huge bore, but to other people, that have not been in that life with you, they might think it to be a very interesting life. Compared to their lives your life experiences might be absolutely amazing. I call it the welcome to my world syndrome. My world is my world and you can not come in unless I allow you to. No matter how hard you try, if I don't want you in my world you are not getting in.

When you do get to look into another person's world that you have never been around, it's like looking into another realm. We all have a tendency to want to take a look at the world from different angles than what our lives have offered. Yes, this would be an interesting title, "The Astounding Adventures of an Ordinary Person from Rural America", or maybe "The Adventures of a City Dweller". I know of one writer that has done well writing about his dating escapades.

So, go for the gusto and tell your story, someone will love to read about your life experiences. If you don't think you're a very good storyteller, surely you know how to do something. How to books are very popular, How To Cook, How To Make Money, How To Cook Brownies, How To Please Your Mate, How To Be A Good Mom, How To Cook A Turkey, How To Be A Good Dad, How To Cook Fried Rice Twenty Different Ways, How To Find A Nursing Home For Your Parents, How To Cook A Blueberry Pie, How To Mentally Block Out Your In-Laws, How To Stay Single, How To Cook Spam, How To Diet, How To Eat Right, How To Save Money, How To Cook Country, How To Stay Beautiful, How To Make Your In-Laws Go Home, How To Write a How To Book.

Ok, so you say these things have been told a thousand times and you would be correct. In year 2005 some of the hottest selling books were diet books. Can we count how many diet books have been printed? I can probably find at least a half dozen diet books around my house. There's a constant stream of diet books and health related books being introduced every year. Inspirational books are also very popular and so are religious based books. Who knows, your way of getting the message out could be the best that has ever been conceived, so put the message out in your words and see how the public responds.

I also like the idea of children's books, twenty to thirty words a page. You wouldn't think that would be so hard to accomplish, at least with those kinds of books it shouldn't be very difficult to spot your mistakes. With very few words per page, surely you would catch the errors after four to five readings.

You may need to co-op your book with a good illustrator though. That's right, you don't have to write or even illustrate the complete book your first time out. If you have a good theme for a children's book you can co-write it first with someone that has more experience than you.

If you want to get motivated to write children's books, go pick up a copy of "The Very Hungry Caterpillar", by Eric Carle. It has sold over twelve million copies. Also, it has been around for decades and is still a top seller. He also has a Brown Bear series along with several other little critter types that seem to be selling well.

I am sure the children's market is as tough as any market to break into, but if you set your goals for that market your chances are as good as the next writer. Children's books also have alternative markets to sell to other than your normal bookstores. If I were writing children's books, I would consider daycare centers, toy stores, medical offices and school libraries in my marketing plans.

What to Publish

Go to Amazon.com or Barnesandnoble.com and look at the 100 best selling titles. Do this for several weeks to get a feel for what is actually selling. You will see a fair share of cookbooks, diet books, health books, how to books, and children's books.

You need to look at writing and selling books as a business, what is hot and what the market is buying. You may have a passion for the nightlife of the Owls, but I doubt you would have many buyers. On the other hand if you wrote a book on how you lost forty pounds from eating possum fat once a day for thirty days, you would probably have a best seller. Maybe another good seller would be, "I Was a Sex Slave to Satan", but I can't get the devil to pay child support. Romance Novels do well also, but that would require a lot of work for a new writer and maybe some experience too.

Don't take your eye off of the ball, remember the object here is to make money and to do that you need to sell what the market is willing to buy. After you establish an income, then it will be much easier for you to write about or research the material that you have a burning desire to do. Speaking of selling books, look at Dan Brown's, "The Da Vinci Code", twenty-five million books in print, in its first two years. Prior to "The Da Vinci Code", Mr. Brown was just another struggling author, with his previous three novels being modestly received by readers. Mr. Brown's success proves that readers will buy books, if the subject matter is interesting.

What to Publish

Another way of starting off writing is with technical manuals, guides and software. This kind of writing is more straightforward with descriptions and sequences compared to trying to tell a story that would hold someone's interest. If you write a very good technical manual or guide, it could be suitable for libraries to include in their current inventory.

Most authors don't think about the public and school libraries as paying customers. If you write a manual that could be beneficial to all citizens, then the library system has a civic duty to keep a copy on hand for all citizens. A good size county might have twenty-four or more branches in their library system. Say two to four copies per branch and how many counties are in each state. You could then double that number when you include public and private school libraries.

I would place overall health and safety guides in this category. If you write a good school play, only schools might pick up something like that. Most county library sites has a place on their web pages to suggest books. That's a good place to start to let the public library systems know what you have to offer them. Don't be bashful, some libraries will even thank you for bringing your book to the attention of their library system.

Could there be anything else out there to publish? The answer is yes, there are more things that can be published. You can try your hand at photo-books for weddings and school yearbooks or you could publish a photo-book of your children. This could also be a good hobby creating photo-books of your children's activities such as ball teams and dance troops.

We also have digital images and the latest craze is to design your own calendar. Personal family calendars makes for a great gift item around Christmas. I think calendars could also be used as a fundraising item for schools, churches or any club you might be associated with. There is always that outside chance that maybe you will be the one that comes up with that special "E.T." calendar that everyone just cannot live without owning one.

When it comes to what can be published the only limitations you have are your own imagination. There are plenty of creative juices within us all, it's just a matter of each individual finding his or her spark to ignite the interest. History is full of ordinary people that have accomplished extraordinary feats. The Wright brothers never went to flying school, but built a plane. So what, you didn't go to writers school, write and publish something any way. If Noah had waited until he graduated engineering school before he built that Ark, the world would have been in big trouble.

From Self-Published Novelist to Best-Selling Author

An interview with Richard Paul Evans

by **Carolyn Campbell**

Richard Paul Evans originally wrote <u>The Christmas Box</u> to show his two daughters he loved them, and to tell his mother he understood her grief in losing a child. Yet through his persistent determination and marketing genius, Evans parlayed his self-published novel into a $4.25 million advance contract from Simon & Schuster and established himself as one of the most financially successful authors of the '90s.

The Christmas Box made history as the only self-published novel to hit #1 on The New York Times best-seller list as a self-published book. It further set a precedent as the only book to simultaneously hit #1 on The New York Times hardcover and paperback best-seller lists. According to The Wall Street Journal, in 1995, The Christmas Box had the highest one-week sales of any book in their list's history.

What do you see as the most important first step in considering self-publishing a book?

First, don't start by considering self-publishing. Becoming self-published is not the easy way to become a published book author, but it is sometimes the only way.

In studying self-publishing, you will see both history and the law of chance aren't on your side. When I decided to self-publish The Christmas Box, no publisher wanted it, yet I sensed that readers wanted it very much. I would definitely begin by submitting the book to traditional publishers through an agent rather than trying to send it to publishers directly.

Are there ways to sense when it is time to shift from seeking traditional publishing to deciding to self-publish? How long did you wait?

You have to listen to your gut instinct. I quit sending The Christmas Box off to publishers really fast. I sent to six publishers. My mail all came back and said the same thing, and even all the local publishers had no interest. You need to listen to what the rejections are saying and ask yourself if they are all saying the same thing. If they suggest changes that make sense to you, as far as making a better book, do it.

But at the same time, realize that if you have something that is a new paradigm the experts often aren't experts. A paradigm pioneer is going to be rejected because it doesn't look like a best-seller. Both The Christmas Box and The Celestine Prophecy didn't look like what was succeeding at the time when they were released. Now everyone wants to see a book that looks like one of those two books.

Are there ways to anticipate whether a particular book is marketable as a self-published book?

One way is what I call the tuna casserole syndrome. Say you have a great tuna casserole recipe. You invite friends over for dinner and they say it's great. If some of the people at your party go out and start making tuna casseroles, that isn't the time to self-market your recipe. But if someone calls back a week after the dinner and says they are coming to get the recipe to start making it for their friends and their friends start calling you for the recipe -- that is when you know you might have something.

Before you decide to self-publish, start sharing your book with people around you -- family, friends and business associates. Be sure you are convinced that you have something special, because it takes a lot of work to take your book outside your own circle. And I would start with agents, not publishers.

Once you have decided that self-publishing might be your route, what financial and artistic considerations should you keep in mind before you begin?
Make sure you have the funds to print, design and market the book. Above all, your book must not look like a self-published book. Ninety-nine percent of the time, readers, distributors and booksellers can pick out a self-published book. If your book does not look as good as a book published by Doubleday, which is who you are competing with, don't bother.

How significant is book design in contributing to book sales in self-publishing?

There is a phrase called "nephew art." This is where someone says, "I had a nephew who was a hippie van painter -- I'll let him design my book cover." Sad to say, lots of time when you get a friend to do illustration, you kill yourself in the market. Friend illustrations are too often sappy and cheap and don't compete on a level with national publishers.

When I decided to self-publish The Christmas Box, I decided on a very simple cover design with no illustrations. When Doubleday called, they told me mine was one of the most attractive self-published books they'd ever seen.

I'd suggest hiring an advertising agency or graphic design firm to do your book -- it's worth the money to make your book look like more than it is. If you put out $5,000 to print your book, it's worth $1,000 to make it look right. It's easily worth 10% to 20% of the printing cost to make the book look its best because if you make it look wrong you waste all of your money.

Once your book is designed and ready to market, what is the next step?

You have to have adequate distribution. Call the bookstores and ask which distributors they are working with. Distributors can make more money with your self-published book than with a national book coming down, so they are your sales force. Distributors are locally-based, so call the ones near you and ask a lot of questions.

How do distributing and marketing intersect?

If your book looks good, and you have the promotion and design, you will get more distribution. Back to the tuna casserole again. Say you walk into a store and want them to sell your tuna casserole. They'll ask why they should sell yours when they have a deli there. You tell them it's because you are doing a radio show and telling people to come to their store. You are making them money.

The only question in all marketing is "what's in it for me?" You have to give them a reason to sell your book. A crucial aspect that I learned is that there are two sales that take place -- one to the bookseller and one to the consumer. With The Christmas Box, consumers forced the booksellers to take the book in. It hit #2 on The New York Times best-seller list, but was only in 20% of the bookstores, so every bookseller in America was looking for The Christmas Box. When I went to the ABA show, booksellers told me, "You are the guy that ruined our Christmas."

How important is self-promotion when self-publishing a book?

It matters ultimately. Someone has to care about your book, and if you are very lucky, you'll have a publisher and a publicist who care a great deal. If you're not willing to work for it, the publisher will usually back out and back down to your level... and you will limit what you have. At the ABA show during my first year with The Christmas Box, I sat next to a young woman who also had a self-published book. While my book was doing very well, hers wasn't selling at all. I thought her concept sounded good, so I was curious about her lack of sales. As we talked she said she wouldn't go on radio shows because she hated her voice, wouldn't do newspaper interviews because she gets too nervous, and wouldn't do book signings because she hates to speak in public. She was doing absolutely nothing and had an excuse for everything. I soon decided she didn't want her book [to sell] that much.

What avenues of self-promotion did you find to be most effective and accessible?

Radio is the easiest and most accessible. In the beginning at least, it's too difficult to get on TV. But there is always a little 1,000 watt radio station where you can call and asked to be interviewed. Now, when I go on tour, I do 20 cities and there is someone to meet me at every airport. But in the beginning, I did it in my own car, got a hotel room close to the airport, got a rental car and started driving. You can buy radio station guides, or find them at the library or on the Internet. I'd look for talk stations and ask to be on their show. I'd get up in the morning and do interviews. When I wasn't touring, I did a lot of radio interviews by phone at my home.

When I first started, I was trying to get a local independent chain to sell my book. They were not real interested until I told them I had already ordered a billboard campaign. They were a lot more interested when they understood that I had put as much money behind promoting my book as I put into printing it.

In the beginning, I put $7,000 into the Utah market. I sold my book for $4.95 and put $1 into promotion for each book I sold. Initially, I hired a local publicist at between $1,000 and $1,500/month. It's worth it if you have the money. It's also important to realize just how big the United States is. You can drop $100,000 in marketing and not make a dent.

With the small window of opportunity that you have to be successful and get noticed, the best strategy is to be a big fish in a small pond. Focus your money on a local market. If The Christmas Box had been brought out nationally, it never would have sold among 80,000 other titles. In the first year, I concentrated on the Walden Books just in Utah. The other regions saw our sales record and realized The Christmas Box was not on their list, and they ordered it for the next year.

What advice would you give self-published authors about book tours?

Book tours can be tremendously valuable sales tools. If you are going out to sell your book as a self-published author, tell why you wrote the book, the effect it had on you and others, and give people reasons to buy the book.

I'm the first author I've ever seen hand out fliers at book signings. To help keep people from shying away from approaching an author sitting at a table, hand them a flier, tell them about the book, give little quotes or testimonials. But don't plan to go to bask in great glory. Remember that this is not an ego trip. If you think it is, you will get eaten up emotionally. Always go on tour to work. A lot of authors drop out of touring. But remember, you have to pay the price if your book and the message you are sharing really matters to you.

What do you see as your most innovative promotional strategy?

A really defining moment happened at the Mountain Plains book show. I wanted to meet the booksellers, who were all out meeting the well-known authors who were brought in by the publishers. The booksellers would get their books autographed and then get back in line behind another established author. I could see that I was really missing the audience here.

It suddenly hit me that if I didn't care about this book, who would? I noticed there was one empty seat at the end of the table where the big-name authors were sitting. I went and sat down in that chair with my books. One of the organizers saw me. I could tell by the look on her face that she intended to ask me to leave. When she came up to me, I looked up and asked, "Am I late?" A bit flustered, she asked, "May I get you some water?" I saw her the next year, after The Christmas Box became a best-seller with a $4.25 million advance from Simon & Schuster. She said I'd come quite a ways and I thanked her for not throwing me out. She asked, "What did it hurt?"

What was your greatest challenge in self-promoting your book?

Let me say that my failures were the best thing that could happen to me. If I'd gotten a publisher right off, I wouldn't have the success I have now. Because I had to promote it myself, I learned how to become market-driven. I needed to be real honest about the dynamics. When I saw what happened locally, I knew that if I could duplicate that nationally, I could have the number one best-seller in history.

Along the way, I discovered it's very difficult to get national media attention for fiction. Talk show hosts feel that fiction isn't intriguing or relevant enough for them to sit down and talk about it. Eighty percent of the books featured on talk shows are nonfiction, where they can talk about relationships or dyads or near-death experiences. They feel that asking a fiction author to "tell me what your book is about," doesn't make a good interview.

Luckily, I had a story behind my book (his mother losing a child to death) that made it interesting to the press.
When you become market-driven, you find out who likes your book and who your market is. I crossed paths with the author of a book called Twelve Golden Threads, about the lessons learned tying quilts. She was having meetings and book signings with quilting clubs. I thought her focus was a good move. Once you find the basic example of who is buying your book, that is the key to success on a larger scale.

When do you recommend beginning self-promotion efforts?

Start a year in advance to plan the best time to release your book. Author Dave Baldacci (Absolute Power, The Winner, Total Control) released his book this year in mid-December. The year before, he released a book on Jan. 1. Why Jan. 1?

Because all the major guns are dropping their books in November and December. Michael Crichton came out with his book Feb. 1. Lots of books come out during Christmas, when all the sales are.

Why did you write The Christmas Box? Why should anyone write a book?

I wrote The Christmas Box because it mattered to me. In the beginning, publishing wasn't a consideration. The book was written with all of my heart for my two daughters. If the only result was that they understood that their father loved them, that would have been enough. If my mother was the only one who read it and she knew that I understood her pain over losing a child, that would have been enough. The Christmas Box worked because it mattered to me. Write something because it matters.

Richard Paul Evans - http://www.richardpaulevans.com

Carolyn Campbell carolync@sisna.com has published more than 600 articles in national magazines. Her articles have also been published internationally in China, Japan, Germany, England, Denmark and Australia. Campbell is the author of,
Together Again: True Stories of Birth Parents and Adopted Children Reunited
Love Lost and Found: True Stories of Long-Lost Loves-Reunited at Last
Reunited: True Stories of Long-Lost Siblings Who Find Each Other Again

Where to Get Published

There are several places that offer print on demand publishing. I Universe is one and it has been around a good while and has a good reputation of getting quality work out and into the retail chain. You can visit I Universe at www.iuniverse.com. It wouldn't hurt to spend some time looking at what they have to offer, browse the site, read and study their rules and price structure. It may cost you more to get published with I Universe than with some others that I will mention here. So, if you're not dead broke, it wouldn't hurt to give them a good look. If you're an author that can't get to first base with a traditional publisher, your work should at least see the light as for getting published. It will of course depend on the quality of your work and the demand of your product whether you see sells of any significance.

BookSurge is another self-publishing and print on demand publisher that was recently bought out by Amazon. I haven't seen any major benefits to the author to publish through them though. Another print on demand is Café Press, it's much cheaper than I Universe, but does not offer nearly as much as for editing, reviewing and getting the product into the retail chain and as far as I know has no close ties with any major bookstores. What it does have to offer though is a site that has been around for some time and its own group of online stores where you can also market and sell T-shirts, sweat-shirts, coffee mugs and a decent array of other items including your book, music and such.

So, if you have a product with a theme and would also like to market other items with your book, the price is right to setup your first online store. The quality of their products is good and delivery time is good also. Located at http://www.cafepress.com. Your work might not make anyone's bestseller list being published here, but it's a good place to start especially if you just want to see your work in a quality book form. Your book can grow from here and make it to the retail chain. I have a journal in this category, http://www.cafeshops.com/the_mystical. If you care to you can go to the site for some ideas.

There are many more print on demand publishers, if you need to find more than I'm offering you, do a Google search or use any web browser, search for Print on Demand Publishers.

Now for the print on demand publisher that I'm currently using, it's Lulu Press Incorporated located at www.lulu.com it's a good site with plenty to offer, whether it's books, music, imaging, poems or calendars, there's something for everyone. At Lulu you can create your own work and have it printed in book form at zero cost to you until you buy a copy. Lulu only charges you twenty-percent commission on your profits. So, for any product you sell on the site you get eighty-percent profit. That's a good percentage going to the creator. I sincerely don't believe you'll find a better deal in publishing.

The downside is that Lulu will not hold your hand and baby-sit you. They give you the tools and the place to create your product for free. There is support through the forums for your many questions though. The other users on the site will answer questions and offer good advice if you're nice.

Lulu does offer more, like editing and help with book covers and such for a fee. They also offer ISBNs that you have to have to get your book listed with Books in Print. The ISBN number is also where your barcode is derived from. For you to sell your book in bookstores, you will need the ISBN and bar code.

Lulu offers two levels of ISBN service, the basic level will cost you only $34.95 and gets you a scanable bar code on the back cover of your book. Your book listed in Books In Print, the searchable database that librarians, booksellers, publishers, students, faculty, researchers, library patrons and bookstore customers use to find the titles they need. It also gives you the ability to take a number of your books into local bookstores for them to sell. The ISBN basic service only makes your book accessible to retail booksellers. Your book will not be listed as current inventory in retail bookstores unless they decide to place an order for stocking purposes or a book distributor picks up your book. Once your book is in that huge database, there are ways of getting your title noticed..

The second level is their ISBN global expanded distribution service for $149.99 and if you buy the basic service first you can upgrade later to the ISBN global for the difference.

This is where their services are really good and are cheaper than their competitors. What you get is the same features of the basic ISBN service, a scanable barcode on the back cover, your book listed in Books in Print and the ability for local bookstores to sell your book. The book will be entered into Ingram's database, the largest U. S. book wholesaler. This gets your book into the same wholesale channels as the major traditional publishing houses.

Typically the ISBN global service gets your book listed in the major online booksellers inventory such as Amazon, Barnes and Noble and Books A Million. However each bookseller has the final say as to the inventory that gets selected. In other words just because you purchased the ISBN global service it doesn't necessarily mean that your book will be listed with every online bookstore. But for a new unknown author your chances are better than with a traditional publishing house.

With ISBN global you have to set your discounted retail pricing structure. Lulu will walk you through the retail pricing option, enabling librarians, bookstore buyers and independent storeowners the ability to order copies at discount prices directly from Lulu, unlike some print on demand publishers. Some print on demand publishers only offer their titles to bookstores at short discount prices of twenty percent off through the major wholesalers, making it unprofitable for independent bookstores to carry their titles. Lulu always offers your book to bookstores at regular discount prices. The same price structure the major stores would get.

Lulu print on demand partner uses a high quality, acid-free, book- grade of opaque paper stock. All books with trims sizes of 6"x9" or smaller are printed on a 55# natural shade opaque. Larger books are printed on 50# white. Paperback covers are printed on a bright white 80# cover stock.

When you purchase an ISBN global service to have an opportunity at having your book listed with online bookstores, Lulu will require you to purchase a proof-book before releasing your book to the distributor. You should go over your proof copy meticulously to make sure there are no errors, before you approve your book for global distribution. If you discover you need to make a change after you have approved the book, you must pay a non-negotiable change fee of $79.95. This fee is set by the distributor and cannot be waived.

How to Get Published

There are several different ways at going about the task of getting your first book together. It isn't advisable to go straight down the line of creating page one until the finished product. That method hardly ever works for a seasoned writer. The best method I have found is to write whatever comes to you and then go over the material several times to sort out the order in which it should be arranged. It's also advisable to submit your finished product to someone for editing and reviewing. If you can't afford a good editor in the beginning, use your family and friends for at least proofreaders.

After you start writing seriously you'll soon see how easy it is to over look mistakes on the material that you stare at too long. Even after you have gone through your work twenty times and you feel it has to be perfect now; chances are someone else will see stuff right from the start you have over looked several times. Don't let it get you down if you find you're making more than your fair share of mistakes, you will get better in time. There will be some learning curves to overcome, like with anything new.

Don't limit yourself to just books and poems. Lulu has a good music section on their site also. You may discover that you have a talent for writing music. With the collaboration setup with other people using the Lulu site, you do not have to be a member of a band to make music, you just need to be able to contribute to the cause.

I live in North Carolina and I co-wrote a nice little song with a fellow (Jimsi) that lives in California. We never even talked to each other, we sent messages and ideas back and forth, through the Lulu collaboration process and some e-mails. I believe the song came out pretty good, it's called Panther Town and is located at www.cafepress.com/panthertown it has a one-minute preview if anyone cares to go to the site and check it out. I'm not sure where the lead guitarist and drummer for that piece reside, but it was all done through the web at www.lulu.com. So search for your talent, there must be something that you can do, to at least contribute to part of a finished product. One of the great things about the Lulu site is the collaboration ability. If you have a great idea, someone else may have the talent to finish the product.

Ok, you have arrived at the www.lulu.com site and it looks kind of Greek to you, now the question is where to start. The first thing to do is get registered and setup your account information. It's painless and Lulu doesn't ask too many questions and they don't ask for any money or a credit card number. So, no one should have a problem with getting registered. The (Sign Up) button is on the home page second line, blue lettering, underneath Browse. On the top bar you'll see a button for Community, I would suggest starting here and getting familiar with the forums. The forums are a handy place to start browsing.

There are several headings under forums, Lulu Support, where you can ask questions for help from the staff when publishing through Lulu. There are other places on the site for specific questions that can be answered by the support team for questions with ISBN, royalties and purchasing. There is also a link to (take the Lulu publishing tour) on the Home Page. It's a flash tour that will walk you through the five steps of getting your book published on Lulu. I highly recommend going through the flash tour several times to get familiar with the publishing process. After going through the flash tour, I suggest going through some of the help nodes. On the Home Page to the far top right is the Help tab. When you click on the Help tab you'll see several topics, the book formatting and book covers FAQ's are a good place to begin with. You should be able to absorb enough of knowledge from these to get you off to a good start.

Now, let's go back to the Home Page and to the forums. Go to Community and then to the Support Forums, and to the Lulu Creator Forums, here you will find several other forums Writer's Word, Image Magic, Music Makers, and Calendar Daze. Under all of these forums are yet more sub forums on just about any topic you might have a question on or you could start your own topic of your choice. Under Writer's Word you'll find stuff like book fairs and up and coming events. You will see other users asking questions between each other and giving out suggestions and offering free advice.

You'll also find authors that would just like for someone to look at their work and give them some kind of input on their material. The critics are house trained and do not bite too hard, so throw your work out there for some feedback. It never hurts to have an extra pair of eyes view your work, regardless of how many times you have gone over it.

After you have gotten familiar with www.Lulu.com it will be time to upload your book or material to the site. On the top left side of the home page is a blue tab labeled (Publish) click on the (Publish) button, this brings you to Start a New Project page with several options, Paperback Book, Hardcover Book, CD/DVD, Digital Media, Brochure, Image, Calendar and e-Book. Here you decide what kind of project you will be starting. This is where your ongoing projects reside. Since you have not started a project yet, click on the (Paperback Book) button. Now you have arrived at the Publish a Paperback Book page, here you'll see several choices Title: Lulu Category: Category: (for refined searching) Copyright Year: Copyright Notice: Edition: and Description. This is your Data Page, you begin by entering the title of your book and then the category and the sub category. All of these are important factors for a successful book. You need to put a lot of thought on the title of your book. A title with a sub title and maybe two sub titles could have a huge impact on sales of your book, if done correctly.

Next select a category and sub category, if you make a bad selection here your book could be virtually impossible to find in an online bookstore. A self-published author must keep in mind that their initial sales will be coming through the Internet bookstores. Next is the year your material was copyrighted in, with new stuff the copyright year would be this year. Now enter a good description of your book, something that would make people want to read your book, do not go overboard though you have enough room for 1024 characters, with spaces. When you have finished with the description choose your audience Children, Everyone, Teen or Mature and then click the button labeled (Save and Continue) you will then be congratulated for successfully creating your book and will be instructed to upload your content via the (Upload File) button.

A window will appear with a (Browse) button. Click on the browse button and go to the folder on your computer that has the file that contains your manuscript, click on the file, and then click on open. Your file should appear in the window beside your (Browse) button, now click upload. The next message should tell you the file has been added to your book successfully. Next click on the Save & Continue button.

You're now at the (Publish a Paperback Book) page and you will see several options for the size of your book Select your book size. The size you choose must be the same size as your original document. If the original document that you uploaded was formatted at 8.5 x 11 then that is the size you must choose. The system will not resize your original document from 8.5 x 11 to 6 x 9. The system might attempt to resize your document, but it will not come out right. Then click Save & Continue. The converter will convert your document to a PDF file, it could take a few minutes to a couple of hours, depending on how complicated your file is. When the converter finishes, you'll have an opportunity to view your file, click on the Preview print-ready PDF button. If all looks ok Approve & Continue.

Next is Colors: black and white pages (with color covers) and then Binding: Perfect-bound (paperback) would be the typical choices. Note you could go with full color pages (with color covers), but in most cases it would be cost prohibited and your book would not qualify for the global distribution program.

The production cost of setting up a book is $4.53 plus .02 per page black and white and .15 per page color. You could do a color page book and go with the basic ISBN with direct sales to bookstores. The coil-bound covers also are not offered with the retail distribution package. The only books that qualify for global distribution are paperback 6 x 9 and 8.5 x 11 with black and white interior.

Next will be the Cover Images section, where you can upload your cover image files for your book. There are two small rectangles, labeled Front Cover and Back Cover. If you have a cover already designed click the browse button for the front cover and go to the file on your computer, open the file. The file with your front cover should appear in the window beside the browse button, next click upload cover and your front cover will appear. Do the same for the back cover, click on the browse button and find your back cover on your computer and upload it. If you do not have a cover designed yet, you can use a cover from the Lulu gallery. Under the upload cover button is a message that reads, choose gallery image. You can click on that and have several choices of generic covers to choose from. Once the covers are selected click the Save & Continue button. Below your covers you'll have the option to add a back cover photo and description to the Lulu gallery covers.

You also have the option to add a one-piece wrap-around cover, recommended for advanced users only. The one-piece wrap-around cover does give you complete control of your cover and spine. On the plus side, you don't have to fight with matching your spine colors with your front and back covers. On the minus side though, it will be up to you to add your ISBN and barcode to your one-piece wrap-around cover.

Next you choose your font and spine color. Click on the square that says Text Color: (title, author, spine) and then pick a color from the color grid and do the same for the Background Color: (spine, cover). After you have decided on your font and background colors, go to Spine Text to add your title and author's name to your spine. Then choose your Spine Font and Title and Author Font. There's a drop down menu to choose your point size for your spine font and title and author font. If you have chosen covers from the Lulu gallery, go to Cover Options and place a check by, display title on cover and display author on cover. When all looks ok to you, click the Update Cover button. If you do not like your covers you can click back button and redo the covers.

Now you'll be given an opportunity to view your press-ready PDF file and view larger version with crop marks. What you see is what you get, so make sure your cover image is perfect and you don't have anything critical within the crop marks. If all is the way it should be, you can click on the Save & Continue button. Now you get to select the format for your book, print or download or both. Next price your book, you can enter your selling price and let the system calculate your royalties or enter your desired royalty amount and let the system calculate the price of your book. Now the last thing to do is to click on the Complete Publish button. You are now a published author.

Now that your book is published, let's spend a little time getting familiar with the site. Go to the Publish Tab at the top of the page. You'll see your title, click on your title to see the detail page. You can set the availability of your book here, available to the public or available to you only or you could retire your book. If you wanted your book only available to you, so you could direct family and friends to it. You could have them do a search by your content number, Lulu.com/content/ your content number.

Below availability are Ratings & Reviews, you can set it to available, anyone can leave ratings and reviews, no purchase necessary or restricted, only those who purchased this item can leave ratings and reviews. The last option would be to have your book unavailable for ratings and reviews. Next you have your view press-ready PDF file and view press-ready PDF cover file. If you click on these files and they won't open in your browser, some files are too large to open in the browser. You can right click on your view press-ready PDF files and save them to your PC to open.

Let's click on the Publish tab again, to the left of your title is your content ID and to the right of your title is the distribution options. You have two options, basic and global distribution. You can purchase basic first to get your ISBN, so you can add it to your copyright page. You can upgrade to global later and only pay the difference.

Let's go back to the Publish tab one more time and click on your title and then scroll down to the bottom of the page. On the bottom right side you'll see either unpublish or create new revision, this is where you go to upload your revised document or PDF file with your ISBN added to your copyright page. You'll see your information page, if nothing needs changing there click on Save & Continue. On the next page you can place a check by your old document to remove it and upload your new document or PDF file. Now finish going through the publishing process again, your cover and everything should stay the same. I would double check my fonts and spine though, to make sure something didn't revert to a default setting that you didn't choose.

The next item to get familiar with is the, My Account tab, at the top of the page. You can set your account preference, email address and password, change content access level, and manage your contact lists, billing and shipping addresses and your remit to and author address. Go to view sales and royalties to keep up with your sales history. The change remission address setting is where you setup how you want to get paid, by Paypal once a month or by check once a quarter. If you choose to be paid by check once a quarter, you'll receive your royalty check about 45 days after the quarter. If you're a US citizen, be sure to include your social security number on your remission form or you won't get paid.

Fine Tuning the Book

Now that you have your book published, you'll need to decide if it's time for you to purchase an ISBN or not. If you don't believe your book is ready for an ISBN at present or you might not have the money available to you to purchase it, you can wait until later. There's no pressure from Lulu to purchase a distribution package, everything is on your timeframe. The good news is that your book is now ready to be printed in a book format with your name on it. You can order one copy or several copies for you and your family and friends to go through to look for errors or to decide if the layout and all came out as you had envisioned. There will be no demands on you from Lulu to buy anything, including the ISBN. The complete process is in your hands. You're in full control of your destiny. So, take your time to insure that you have produced an excellent book.

If you have ideas in your book that could be stolen though, it wouldn't hurt to go ahead and purchase the ISBN basic to have your copyrighted material registered with Books in Print. With adding an ISBN you are basically time stamping your material with two services, Lulu's and the Books In Print database, in the event that a dispute of some kind were to occur at a later date. This should allow you more time to fine tune your material, and give you some protection.

In fact I think it's best to stay in the ISBN basic mode until the book has gone through all of your scrutinizing and you are one hundred percent satisfied that all is ready for the retail chain. While your book is in the ISBN basic mode and you do find errors after you have received a copy such as fonts doesn't look good or you might decide that you should change line spacing or add more text to the content just proceed to (Publish). Then to (my projects) and edit your book. Then go to the bottom of the page and click on either the unpublish button or create new revision, whichever is displayed. Don't be afraid you'll not lose anything, your ISBN will stay with your project and it will simply reset itself to the draft mode. Then you can edit any changes, remove your old content and upload the new content that has your corrections. Unless you are really methodical I doubt very seriously that you'll get the book right on the first print. I'm sure someone will though, there is always one or two over achievers in every crowd. After you have uploaded your corrected version of the book go back through the publishing process.

It will be very difficult for you to contain yourself and not jump the gun when approving your creation for the final stage. The opportunity to get your product into the retail chain is overwhelming to most new authors. By this point everyone is excited and is tired of waiting for your proof copy to get to you for final examination. But you should hold back and take that one last good look at your proof copy before you hit that approve button for the ISBN global package. Once you approve your ISBN for global distribution, your digital files will be sent to the wholesale distributor, LSI / Ingram Books. It will cost you to make any changes from this point on and you really do not want to send shoddy work into the retail chain.

Even if it delays getting your book out for another month, you really should wait and put your eyes on that final proof. One bit of handy information to keep in mind, is the material that is submitted to the distributor before the 15th of the month usually shows up with the online retail stores by the beginning of the next month. And anything submitted after the 15th usually shows up in the system within six to eight weeks. I set my target between the 10th and 12th of the month to approve for global distribution.

Fine Tuning the Book

I'm not going to pretend to be the all knowing when it comes to writing and publishing. I will give some pointers for beginning writers, such as most paperbacks are done in a 6-inch wide by 9-inch tall format. The 8.5 by 11-inch format are usually used for magazines or technical manuals. I like the font points between 10 and 12 Times New Roman. This book is set up with 12 Times New Roman and custom paper size of 6-inch by 9-inch and line spacing: multiple of 1.2, top and bottom margins of 1.00 inch, outside margin of .75 and inside margin of 1.00 inch, in Microsoft Word.

There are two ways to submit your manuscript to Lulu. You can upload your document and let Lulu's converter convert your file to a PDF file or you can create your own PDF file to upload. With either way you'll still have to go back to your original file to add your ISBN to your copyright page. If you choose to upload your document you need to use page breaks in your document instead of hitting the enter key to start a new page. If you don't use page breaks the converter will not align your pages correctly. You also need to use fonts that are compatible with Lulu. These are the fonts you can use Arial, Book Antiqua, Bookman Old Style, Century, Courier, Garamond, Palatino, Tahoma, Times New Roman, Verdana and Symbol. Serif fonts are best for printed documents. Use serif fonts like Garamond, Times New Roman and Palatino for blocks of body text.

The other option for submitting your manuscript to Lulu, is to cerate and upload your own PDF file. Creating your own PDF file will give you more control over your font selection and the layout of your book. You can use any fonts you like, but you must embed the fonts in the PDF file before you upload it to Lulu. If using Acrobat Distiller, from the settings menu select Edit Adobe PDF setting. The general settings are displayed, click the fonts folder and select Embed all Fonts.

Adobe Acrobat Distiller, the default page setting is 8.5" x 11". To create a PDF of another size, you must change the PDF settings in Acrobat Distiller by following these instructions. From the settings menu, select Edit Adobe PDF settings. The general settings are displayed. In the default page size fields, enter the desired width and height of your document, click save as and enter a descriptive name for the job options file.

If your document is a black and white book, make sure the print settings in Acrobat Distiller are set for black and white. If you can't afford Acrobat Distiller, my favorite shareware is PDF Creator. Before you install PDF Creator, you need to install a PostScript Print Driver that has custom page sizes. I use HP LaserJet 5/5m Postscript. Install your Postscript Driver, set as the default printer and go to paper and setup a custom page size. Then install PDF Creator and set it as the default printer with your custom page size. (See page 104)

Basic Book Covers

Your book cover should be completely separate from your main document. You will upload your cover file (s) in a separate step of the publishing process. Lulu does not offer inside cover printing. You have two options for uploading your book cover. You may upload separate front and back covers, or you may upload a single one-piece (wrap-around) cover. Cover files that are uploaded separately must be JPG, GIF or PNG files of at least 300 DPI. One-piece (wrap-around) cover files must be PDF. You may not use a word document as your cover file.

You don't need a high-end graphics program to do a basic book cover. If you have Microsoft PowerPoint that comes with most new computer systems, you can make a nice looking high quality cover. I set my covers up with PowerPoint. First I choose a blank presentation, then a square blank slide layout and click on ok and go to page setup. I set my page size at 6.375 x 9.75 to allow for full bleed, in pixel size your page should be 1913 x 2925 for 300 DPI, which is basically 3 times your inch size to attain your 300 DPI. I then work with a 20% scale that does fine for me. Next right click on that page and go to background, now I choose my color for background fill and click on apply to all. With this procedure I now have a solid colored book cover. If I want to change my cover to a dual colored cover I can.

Right click on your cover and then go to background, that will bring you back to background fill. Click on the down arrow and go to fill effects and choose two colors. You now have two color bars, color 1 and color 2 with several shading styles you can play around with until you find a combination of colors that you are satisfied with. You can now insert text or a picture with your cover, go to the insert button at the top of the program and select insert picture or text. If you insert a picture you go to the file on your computer; open it and presto it pops onto the book cover. You can then size the picture to your satisfaction. You can fill the entire page with your picture, if it's a high resolution picture and then add your title, sub title and authors name over the picture for a very nice looking cover.

For the text, go back to insert, then text, you will see a down pointing arrow. Position the arrow to where you would like for your text to begin, hold down your left mouse button and then draw a block for your title and name. You could leave the title and author's name off of the cover and let the Lulu publishing process add these for you. You should now have a basic book cover that is ready for the press. Now that you have your book cover designed you need to save it, first save your file as a .PPT file and then go back and save it again as a .PNG file. It's important to have both kinds of files to work with. You can come back and make changes to your cover in the .PPT format and you'll need the .PNG format to upload the cover to Lulu.

Marketing Your Book

Once your book hits the bookstore websites such as Amazon, Barnes & Noble, Books A Million and others, you will need to do some work yourself to insure that your book cover image and description is in place at all sites. To add text content or a cover image to the **Barnes & Noble** site send an email to: titles@bn.com. Always include your ISBN number when you send any message to online bookstores. On the subject line tell them to please add your book cover image and description to ISBN 1411626761. Then go to the body of the message and repeat the message you had on the subject line, include your name, the title and ISBN number.

Next type in Description: below that statement enter or cut and paste the description of your book. Then go to the file for the book cover image and save a copy as your ISBN (1411626761) as a .jpg file and add that file as an attachment. Send this information to Barnes & Noble about every three to four days until they update their database. I've found the best time to send your messages to get a quick response is between 10 AM and 3 PM Eastern Standard Time. If you detect an error in your book's details, such as a misspelled title, author's name or an incorrect retail price for your book, you'll need to send an email to: corrections@barnesandnoble.com.

For **Books A Million** the routine is the same, just send your information to their email address. Go to the website, then to the home page and at the bottom of the page you'll find a place For Publishers. This is where you'll find Books A Million's guide lines for submitting your information to them. It's basically the same setup as Barnes and Noble, send to: content@booksamillion.com.

Another important site to get your information out to, is the independent bookstores, that resides at **BookSense.com**. The online setup is basically the same as the other two and there are several hundred of them, about eight hundred independent bookstores. So to update your information at booksense.com send your content and image attachment file to: staff@booksense.com. Also, if you go to their site you will see a store locator section that has a place where you can browse by state, that has email addresses, websites and phone numbers. You could use this to work up a mailing list or email list and send letters or messages describing what it is that you have to offer. Some of the owners will thank you for bringing your product to their attention, and a hand full will complain and ask you to remove them from your list.

To add your description to **Buy.com,** go to the website and pull up your title, then scroll down to the bottom of the page to the Suggestion Box. Include the title, ISBN, author's name and your books description, then click on the submit button.

To add your cover image and description to Borders, go to **Borders.com**, then to Borders Stores at the top of the page. On the next page go to Customer Care at the top of the page and on the following page go to Guide for Publisher, on the left side of the page.

How to Submit Additional Content
We'll be happy to review any additional content for inclusion on the detail page for your title. Recommended content includes cover art, book synopses, reviews, and author/artist bios. For Text: We can accept just about any format (text, Word, Excel, or Access), but we prefer a text document containing all records.

Format Example:

ISBN/UPC: 10 digits
TITLE:
CONTRIBUTORS: Author, Performer, Illustrator, Narrator (Let us know the relationship)
FORMAT:
RETAIL PRICE:
PUBLISHED DATE:
PUBLISHER NAME:
PAGE COUNT:
AVAILABILITY: Let us know if it is Active, Out of Print, Cancelled, Not Yet Published
EDITION NUMBER:

AGE RANGE:
DESCRIPTION:
AUTHOR/PERFORMER BIO:
REVIEW:
EXCERPT:
SUBJECT/GENRE: Fiction
SUBJECT/GENRE: Mystery
SUBJECT/GENRE: Thriller
SUBJECT/GENRE: Women Detective
SUBJECT/GENRE: New Orleans
END

We can list up to five subjects/keywords to your record.

For Images:
The requirements to submit cover art are as follows:

* Electronically: Saved by the 10-digit ISBN or 12-digit UPC (music and video/DVD), in either JPEG (*.jpg), GIF (*.gif), or TIFF (*.tif) formats. We prefer JPEG or GIF.

* No larger than 150 dpi (dots per inch) and no larger than 250K per image. (The size is very important only if you are emailing the images, otherwise we can work with any size.)

* Images can be submitted via floppy disk, CD-ROM, ZIP Disk, or via FTP.

Where to Send:

Please send all additional content to us at one of the following locations:

Borders Data Integrity

100 Phoenix Drive

Ann Arbor, MI 48108

Email: acquisitions@bordersgroupinc.com

FTP: please contact us at the email address above for specific directions.

If you have any questions or concerns, or if you would like to discuss other methods of submission please email us at the address above.

Submitting Titles for Store Consideration

If you are interested in having your title stocked in a Borders store, please send two copies of each title and a cover letter including company address and proposed terms to:

New Vendor Acquisitions

Borders Group, Inc.

100 Phoenix Drive

Ann Arbor, MI 48108

The last online bookstore website we will go over is **Amazon.com**. Their setup is a bit different and more difficult to master. Go to Amazon.com and then to books and scroll down to near the bottom of the page until you see in big bold letters Publishers and Authors. Under that click on Publishers' Guide. Then go to Add Descriptive Content and then to Book Content Update Form fill this form out to the best of your ability. There maybe several places on this form you will not need to fill in don't worry about it. Make sure you get the title, ISBN, the author and description in the correct place. Use Lulu Press Inc. as the publisher and your contact info.

After you finish updating your content into Amazon's database, go back to Publishers' Guide, then to Add Images, then to Cover Art. If you forget how you got to the Publishers' Guide the first time, just go back to the beginning of this section and follow the instructions. Images sent to Amazon must be at least 500 pixels on the longest side at 72 DPI. The book cover image file must be in .JPG or .TIF format, with your ISBN as the name "1254545332.jpg", but it can not be sent as an email attachment. The file will have to be sent using the Internet's FTP (File Transfer Protocol). You'll need to send an email requesting a password and username to ftp-subs@amazon.com. Then go to Google and do a search for FTP shareware, I use FTP Voyager at, rhinosoft.com.

Now it is time to get your book noticed and have some fun in the process. I'm not a literary expert, my expertise is in computer logic and databases. This is the field that I have spent more than a decade pulling my hair out trying to get a grasp of. You might read a description of one of my books and say to yourself, why did he even insert that information in there. That is a given, anyone with half a brain would know it is a given.

Well, guess what, we are not dealing with individuals that have the capacity to think and process logic. What we the self-published authors that have to rely on the Print on Demand process must understand is that our initial contact with our customers will come via the online bookstores. The Internet, the super highways of information, with millions of people out there in cyber land, that are waiting for us to share our hard earned knowledge with them.

If you devise your description with the Internet in mind, you will receive optimum results for your efforts. Here is an example for you. Go to Barnes & Noble and to books, do a keyword search for (work from home) you will eventually find my book " How To Get Published Free " and the higher I'm ranked, the sooner you'll find it. Work from home is not included in my title, but it is included in my description with the purpose of getting more people to find my book by using a popular phrase.

Understanding database logic will be a key ingredient to having any success marketing your book on a shoestring budget. Most of us self-published authors are not going to have a lot of money for marketing. Unlike a traditional publishing house that can spend huge amounts of money advertising a book they think could be a bestseller. The average self-published author will have little to no money to promote their book and must rely on their common sense and use any resource they can seize. Without the proper use and understandings of database logic your title will be thrown into a cyber warehouse along with ten million other titles. Eventually someone might stumble across your title and decide to buy it.

The information that I'm going to share with you is the result of much research and if you apply it correctly it will enhance the odds of your book being noticed by a larger audience. When more people see your title the chances of selling more books will increase and when you sell more books the higher your rankings will climb. Now with a higher ranking even more people will notice your book resulting in selling more books and the cycle goes on. I hope by now you are beginning to understand that having your book listed with online bookstores without some kind of marketing plan, will most likely result in very few sells.

The first thing you need to consider is the title of your book. You really do need to spend a lot of time considering what your title should be named. If you take into consideration that you are dealing with the Internet and that keywords and key phrases are very important to your success. We are not dealing with people walking through a bookstore looking at pretty book covers, we are working within a database program where people insert keywords and key phrases to search for what they want.

So, make your title interesting and use as many key words and key phrases as possible to get your book noticed without going overboard. There is no problem with having a long title on the Internet or a short title with a sub title or even a double sub title if needed. For example let's look at my title " How To Get Published Free: Best in Self-Publishing & Print on Demand: Plus Marketing Your Book on The Internet " the main title is "How To Get Published Free" with two sub titles that are created for maximum exposure. Every word in your title and sub titles is considered keywords or key phrases. With this title you can go to Amazon or Barnes and Noble and type in (how to get published) and find my book or you could type in (book marketing) or (self-publishing) and also find my book. My use of keywords and key phrases has been so successful that you can go to Yahoo shopping and type in how to get published free and find my title at or near the top of a quarter of a million titles, that is exposure.

The second most important thing to consider when working within a database is the description of your book. We are mostly working within two major Internet sites with Amazon as the heavy weight and Barnes & Noble as a distant second, online mine you. If you manage to get your book into the Barnes & Noble stores, then the number one retailer for you would quickly change over to Barnes and Noble.

During my extensive research of online website databases I have come to the conclusion that Barnes & Noble uses the title of your book as well as the description of your book in their database search engines. So you need to keep in mind that your description can be just as important to the success of your book as your title on Barnes & Noble, so word your description accordingly.

I would be a little devious about how I constructed my descriptions though. If you just typed in a hundred bullets of keywords and key phrases someone might get a little suspicious and delete all of your information. All I'm saying is don't go over board and be a pig, but do be discreet and take advantage of your newfound knowledge. If you methodically work the system for what it is, you will be amazed at how far you can take your book with little or no advertising money.

Ok, since we have Barnes and Noble down now we need to work on Amazon. Your title is still considered as keywords and key phrases. Your description is still important here also, but not as keywords and key phrases. Amazon does offer the Search Inside This Book option and uses the info there as keywords and key phrases. To sign up for the Search Inside This Book option, go to Amazon books and pull up your title, look under your book's cover image for Publishers: learn how customers search inside this book, then click on <u>Sign up</u>. Once you sign the Publisher Participation Agreement and are accepted into the program, you'll need to provide Amazon with a physical copy of each book you would like to include in the program.

The next marketing tool you can use on Amazon is the (Tag this product) located above Customer Reviews. If you're the first customer to tag a book your nickname and your comment will appear under (Customers tagged this item with) as (First tag). Your comment can be the last tag also, but that doesn't really help your marketing cause very much. The first tag is your goal, because it will be displayed with the book right above (Customer Reviews). The tags that I normally use are good, very good, must read, excellent and interesting. I have designed my nickname to be noticeable when I mange to be a first tag. You can go to Amazon's best selling 100 books and usually find me as first tag on 12% to 20% of them.

I will appear on some top 100 bestsellers as First tag: <u>excellent</u> <u>(Book Hound)>> Get Published Free</u> on May 25, 2006). That's pretty good exposure being on a major title right above Customer Reviews. The tag comment I used is excellent and my nickname is Book Hound)>> Get Published Free. I designed my nickname to entice potential customers to click on my nickname. When you click on my nickname my Amazon profile will display. I use my profile as another marketing tool. Instead of displaying my ugly mug on my profile, I display my books cover image. So, if anyone gets curious and clicks on my profile, the first thing they will see is my book's cover image.

The web page url I use under my profile is redirected back to my book on Amazon. I have it setup to where a potential customer can get to my book on Amazon from some of the bestsellers. You need to tag more than just the bestsellers though, you need to tag books that are closely related to your book by categories and subject. I suggest tagging the top 25 to 50 titles in any category that is related to your title.

The next marketing tool on Amazon to look at is (So You'd Like to <u>Offer your advice</u>). Go to books on Amazon and type in a key phrase in the search window such as (self-publishing). Then go to the top left side of the page and click on <u>Offer your advice.</u> Follow the instructions to fill the form out. You can add 50 titles to the form. Place your title in the top three and select other titles in categories and subjects related to your title.

Another feature on Amazon you can use as a marketing tool is the (Listmania!) you can add a list of recommended titles. You can have from three to twenty-five titles per list and you can have a dozen or more lists, I suggest you use all twenty-five slots per list. How do you setup your Listmania! List? Go to Amazon and then to books and type a key phrase in the search window, type in how to get published or how to make money. Then click on the go button a Listmania List will show up on the right side of your screen. You will see an option to (Create a Listmania! list) click on this option to start your list. You setup your Listmania by categories and subjects that are closely related to your title.

Do your list as Relevance and as Best-selling, place your book at the top of the list. Go through all of categories and sub categories that are similar to your book and make as many Listmania lists as possible. If you do your Listmania right your book cover image will start showing up as people browse for related topics.

I had a batch of twelve lists that were averaging over a thousand hits a week until it accidentally got deleted. When I setup my list I usually add two or three of the top 100 best selling titles also, sometimes your Listmania list will show up with their page and that gives you more chances of being noticed. When creating your list always add the top seven to ten titles in order for each category.

We have yet another marketing tool on Amazon that we can take advantage of. When you pull up your book up, over on the right side of the screen under (Add to Shopping Cart) there is an option for (More Buying Choices) and at the bottom of this option is a statement (Have one to sell? Sell yours here) this is where you sell copies that you have purchased from Lulu at production cost. When you use this option make sure that you do have those books on hand, so you can ship the books out to your customers within one to two business days.

This is a marketing strategy you could use indefinitely as long as there are customers buying your books from the Amazon Marketplace, you can look at this as a cheap means of marketing. The way I do this is I buy two books from Amazon, which helps my rankings. The cost really is minimal after I receive my payment from Amazon and after their commission and my royalty from Lulu it usually cost me between $1.25 and $1.50 per book after shipping and packaging cost. When sales gets heavy enough for me not to have a need to worry with rankings, then I will buy all of my books from Lulu and make between $8.00 and $9.00 a book. If you set the Amazon Marketplace price for your book about $2.50 below Amazon's price this will entice people to buy it quicker, because that covers their shipping cost.

Another reason to have books on hand to sell through Amazon's Marketplace is when your book first goes on sale on Amazon they will have a very limited supply of your books, maybe one or two copies. Your book will go from usually ships in 24 hours to as long as usually ships in 10 to 13 days, if your customers are placing orders on a regular basis. Eventually Amazon, Ingram and Lightning will catch on and decide that your book could be a good selling book and keep more copies on hand. You can see how this could initially slow down the pace of your sales if customers have to wait 10 to 13 days before the book is shipped. If you have books for sale on Amazon's Marketplace and it says that these books usually ships in 1 or 2 business days, and they are priced just below the price of normal shipping cost, some customers will order from you instead of waiting 2 to 3 weeks for delivery.

We need to work on one more thing with our online marketing and that is how your book is listed and by this I mean what category or subject your book is listed under. Usually your title is associated with just one or two categories and they maybe very vague and have you hidden so deep in the system that no one can find your book. Here is a list of categories from Amazon and every category has sub categories also. Most websites calls these categories while Amazon calls them subjects.

Browse Subjects

Arts & Photography

Design, Museums, Art History....

Audiocassettes

Books on Cassette

Audio CDs

Books on CD

Audio Downloads

Books, Newspapers, Lectures, Comedy....

Bargain Books Outlet

Books Under $5, Books Under $10, Bestsellers, Humor....

Biographies Memoirs

Artists, Educators, Philosophers, Writers....

Business & Investing

Tax Planning, Management, Personal Investing....

Children's Books

Classics, Fairy Tales, Series, How It Works....

Christian Books

Bibles, Catholicism, Protestantism, Fiction....

Marketing Your Book

Browse Subjects

<u>Comics & Graphic Novels</u>

Comic Art, cartooning, Comic Strips, Manga....

<u>Computers & Internet</u>

Web Development, Programming, Certification....

<u>Cooking, Food & Wine</u>

International, Regional, Food Lit....

<u>e-Books</u>

Science Fiction, Favorite Authors, Business....

<u>Entertainment</u>

Music, Television, Movies, Games....

<u>Espanol</u>

Literature, Children's Books, Business....

<u>Gay & Lesbian</u>

Coming Out, Fiction, Relationships....

<u>Health, Mind & Body</u>

Diet, Fitness, Relationships, Self-help...

<u>History</u>

Ancient, Military, United States,

Browse Subjects

Home & Garden

Entertaining, Weddings, Crafts, How-To, Pets....

Horror

Vampires, Ghosts, Erotica, Classics....

Literature & Fiction

Novels, Poetry, Essays, Classics....

Mystery & Thrillers

Detectives, Women Sleuths, Spies....

Nonfiction

Politics, Current Events, Social Sciences, Law...

Outdoors & Nature

Hiking, Field Guides, Fishing....

Parenting & Families

Pregnancy, Babies, Childcare, Eldercare....

Professional & Technical

Medical, Engineering, Law, Finance....

Reference

Atlases, Languages, Careers....

Browse Subjects

<u>Religion & Spirituality</u>

Christianity, Judaism, New Age, Occult....

<u>Romance</u>

Contemporary, Historical, Time Travel, Series....

<u>Science</u>

Biology, Mathematics, Physics....

<u>Science Fiction & Fantasy</u>

Alternate History, Epics, High Tech....

<u>Sports</u>

Coaching, Water Sports, Golf, Baseball....

<u>Teens</u>

Fiction, Fantasy, Social Issues....

<u>Travel</u>

Essays, Europe, Asia, U.S....

<u>Women's Fiction</u>

Domestic Life, Single Women, Mothers & Children....

The points of interest to me would be <u>Reference</u>, then

<u>Publishing & Books</u>, <u>Writing</u> and last <u>General</u>.

Browse Reference

General

Almanacs & Yearbooks

Atlases & Maps

Audio Books

Business Skills

Calendars

Careers

Catalogs & Directories

Consumer Guides

Dictionaires & Thesauruses

Education

Encyclopedias

Etiquette

Foreign Languages

Fun Facts

Genealogy

Large Print

Law

Browse Reference

Publishing & Books

Quotation

Spanish-Language Reference

Study Guides

Test Prep Central

Words & Language

Writing

Related Categories

Bargain Books

Foreign Language Calendars

LOOK Inside! Reference Books

Related Products

Encyclopedias & Dictionaries

Foreign language Software

Test Prep Software

You can request for your title to be associated with other sub categories to enhance the marketing efforts for your book. My book was originally setup on Amazon under the subjects of Language Arts / Linguistics / Literacy, and I don't believe those are very high on the average person's browsing list. You can have your title associated with up to ten categories or sub categories. So I sent an email to Amazon requesting a change. To this address: Book-dept@amazon.com this is a copy of what I requested.

Would you please associate my book
How to Get Published FREE: and Make Money
ISBN 1411604091, under these subject listings.
1. Subject; Reference, Publishing & Books
2. Subject; Reference, Publishing & Books, General
3. Subject; Reference, General
4. Subject; Business & Investing, General
5. Subject: Business & Investing, Reference
6. Subject; Reference, Writing
7. Subject; Reference, Writing, General
8. Subject; Reference, Writing, Technical

They gave me # 2 , Reference / Publishing & Books / General

Amazon's powers to be didn't give me all that I requested though, but my book is now in a much better category than where it started off at. This bad category listing was due to my fault of not studying the category structure well enough to know exactly where my book should have been listed to begin with. So study this list well and make an informed decision as how to list your book before you make your final approval and enter into the retail distribution system with your global ISBN. I sent this message to Barnes and Noble to: corrections@barnesandnoble.com

Would you please associate my title with the following subjects and category.

ISBN 1411604091
How to Get Published FREE: and Make Money

1. Reference
2. Reference; English Language Reference
3. Reference; Writing
4. Reference; Writing, Creative Writing
5. Reference; Writing, General & Miscellaneous
6. Business & Investing
7. Business & Investing, General & Miscellaneous
8. Business & Investing, Personal Finance & Investing

I basically got everything I asked for at Barnes and Noble.

Services for New Writers

In this section I will be introducing you to people who are in business to help you get through the book publishing process. There will be a huge learning curve for most new writers and this business of self-publishing can be overwhelming with so much to learn on your own. Some of these services may seem contradictory or even duplicated at times by others, but the purpose is to give you the writer choices. If you have several choices to choose from, then you will most likely find someone you will feel comfortable with to help you get your project finished.

Lotus Books

<u>Publishing Services,</u> LotusBooks.net

Self-publishing can be hard, Lotus Books publishing services can make it easy. What could be more simple than emailing us your completed and edited single-spaced manuscript word document, your bio, photo and cover color & art specifications, when applicable? Since we work with speed and precision, not only can your hard-copy (soft-cover) book literally be in your hand in a few short weeks; you also have the capability to bulk order your book at a greatly reduced rate, which is what we recommend because it is simply more cost effective. Many self- published authors prefer to buy their book in bulk, sell it in their own through book signings, fairs, speaking engagements, their web site, etc... setting their own price and making a noticeable better profit than what most major publishing houses offer. Thus the reason more and more authors are turning to self-publishing. Depending on your individual publishing and selling needs, your book may be hard cover or soft cover, and printed with Xerox Docutech sheet fed and web heat set and cold set web press on.

Lotus Books

<u>Publishing Services,</u> LotusBooks.net

50#, 55#, or 60# paper. Size capabilities range from 5.5" x 8.5", 6" x 9", 7" x 9" inch, 7" x 10" and 8.5" x 11" The above is for bulk orders of 100 or more, and is the most cost effective, only dollars per book!

Lotus Books also offers a $99.00 print-on-demand package. This package is perfect for authors wishing to purchase/sell 100 copies of their book, or who are not yet ready to purchase in bulk and sell on their own.

View our various publishing packages (below), then email your Completed manuscript, and get your free no-obligation quote. Please note we require a partial or full payment before we begin work on your book as this ensures us we are only working with writers who are serious about getting published. For our and your protection, we also require authors to sign any necessary paper work. Currently, we accept money orders, bank checks, cashiers checks, and personal checks, only. Please allow 7-10 days for personal checks to clear.

Lotus Books

Basic POD Package #1

Price $99.00*

Package #1 provides the author with one digitally printed hard-copy (soft-cover 6 x 9 or 8.5x 11.00) print-on-demand version of their book, a Lotus Books created full-color 300 DPI cover, and a free on-line storefront, which we arrange through Lulu Inc., a reputable digital print-on-demand resource, where the author can direct his/her readers/customers to purchase additional copies, at the price he/she sets (printer set-up cost and small printer royalty automatically deducted from each purchased book. The remainder of the author-controlled profit is your as you set the price!). Author retains their copyright, and is paid quarterly. For an additional fee marked by the printer, author has the ability to order an ISBN, have their book listed in Books in Print, & offered for sale at various major online bookstores. We believe this package is great for individual or lesser orders, and not economically practical for authors looking to buy in bulk.

- Prices starting at $99.00, Cost depends on book length.

Lotus Books

<u>The Bulk Seller Package #2</u>

Price: starts at $99.00*, Depends on book size, page count, author design preference, how many books you wish to order in bulk, etc. Bulk is better because it is dramatically less expensive (just dollars) per book!

We format your completed manuscript into an acceptable book format, create your full-color 300 DPI cover, and arrange you to get the best price possible on your bulk purchase. This package allows us to offer you your book at rates that are often 50% (or less) than what you will pay for a book from package #1.

Unlike package #1, books from this package do not include POD identifier ID on the back cover, to which some authors find this inclusion objectionable.

Send manuscripts to: editor@MelanieSchurr.com
And get your free no-obligation quote.
Lotusbooks.net

Lotus Books

Publishing Services,   LotusBooks.net

Lotus Books (LotusBooks.net) was founded in 2003 by former newspaper columnist, Melanie Schurr, who has been a 7+ year. Weekly contributing writer for Daily Wisdom, which is sponsored by The Gospel Communications Network, the most popular Christian Web sites on the Word Wide Web. The purpose of LotusBooks.net is to assist writers who seek to be self-published, yet feel they do not have the time, know-how or resources to do so. At Lotus Books, we work hard so you don't have to!

Contact:
Lotus Books
PO Box 770462
Naples, Fla. 34107

Editor@MelanieSchurr.com
LotusBooks.net

Mark Brooks

Science Fiction, Fantasy & Historical Illustrator.
e: brooks.art@tesco.net
w: http://www.pen-paper.net/gallery.php?artist=Mark_Brooks
t: 01928 820100
m: 07963 512852
a: 6 Great Riding, Norton Cross, Runcorn, Cheshire, United Kingdom WA7 6SL.

Please take a look at my gallery for a comprehensive selection of the work I produce. I have had 5 years experience since leaving university and was formally trained as a Natural History Illustrator. Since then most of my work has been for role playing games & book covers. Usually I will negotiate a rate depending on how long the work is going to take me. International work is not a problem and most of my clients are in the USA. CD's or electronic files can be sent to supply finished artwork.

Please visit:
http://www.pen-paper.net/gallery.php?artist=Mark_Brooks

Mark Brooks

Science Fiction, Fantasy & Historical Illustrator.

e: brooks.art@tesco.net

w: http://www.pen-paper.net/gallery.php?artist=Mark_Brooks

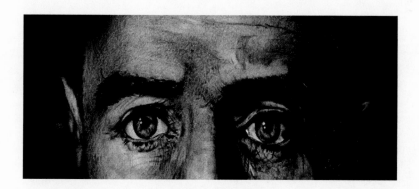

Mark Brooks

Science Fiction, Fantasy & Historical Illustrator.

e: brooks.art@tesco.net

w: http://www.pen-paper.net/gallery.php?artist=Mark_Brooks

Please visit http://www.pen-paper.net/gallery.php?artist=Mark_Brooks

Mark Brooks

Science Fiction, Fantasy & Historical Illustrator.

e: brooks.art@tesco.net

w: http://www.pen-paper.net/gallery.php?artist=Mark_Brooks

ManuscriptEditing.com

<u>Lynda Lotman</u>

Manuscript Editing - Fiction & Nonfiction
Serving publishers, agents, and writers – mainstream genre,
trade, and academic – since 1976. References are provided on
site. 2,500+ credits: books, articles, theses, and dissertations.
Coordinator of an international network of editors and writers
that also includes legal, medical, scientific, and technical
specialists. Services include copyediting, developmental
editing, proofreading, critiques, query letters, book proposals,
writing assistance, mentoring, ghostwriting, typesetting, book
design, indexing, and publicity/promotions.
http://www.manuscriptediting.com
Lynda Lotman
www.manuscriptediting.com

ManuscriptEditing.com

Lynda Lotman

Freelance Network Coordinator

www.englishedit.com

www.thesisproofreader.com

www.apawriting.com

www.dissertationadvisors.com

www.statisticstutors.com

www.book-editing.com

www.writingnetwork.com

Editors and How to Choose One

By Audrey Owen

You've chosen your topic, done your research, and written your book. You may even have contracted graphics and layout. You believe you are ready to publish, and Print on Demand technology makes it possible for you to rush in and do just that.

There's good news and bad news.

The good news is that you absolutely can publish what and when you like.

The bad news is, so can anyone else, and discerning buyers know that. Many are rightfully wary of self-published books.

So how do you make your book stand out in the world of self-published books?

You provide excellent information and you present it flawlessly.

That is where the editor comes in.

It's unfair that you are judged not on your knowledge of widgets, or yoga, or dream interpretation, or children under seven, or financial planning, but on your spelling and grammar, but it's true.

Think of a bride all dressed for her wedding. What is most important? I'd argue it's the character and personality of the bride. But if she shows up with ketchup on her dress or mud on her shoes, what will everyone be thinking through the ceremony?

You may be the most brilliant and insightful person ever to publish a book, but if your writing is less than pristine, you will not sell many books. Sure, you may be able to get a few under the radar of people who buy without cracking the cover, but you won't get the repeat sales. And you won't get the unexpected gold mine of unsolicited reviews. And you won't get the best recommendation of all, word of mouth.

Trade publishers ensure their authors produce the best books possible by hiring editors. Every trade book you have ever read had gone through at least four stages of editing.

Once someone in acquisitions decides the book has potential, an editor does a substantive edit. The editor reads the whole manuscript and looks for ways to improve it on a global level. Did you include all the information you needed? Is your point clear? If it's fiction, are characters, plot, setting and theme working together in the best possible way? The editor writes Fix Notes to the writer, suggesting changes. There may be several rounds of substantive editing before moving on.

The next round is line editing. The editor looks at wording, not for grammar and spelling, but for elegance and power. The editor asks, "Is this the best possible way to say this?"

When the writer and editor agree that everything is said as well as it possibly can be said, the work receives a copy edit. This is when the spelling and grammar are checked. Finally, a proofreader double-checks for spelling and grammar and layout issues.

With all that attention to words in the trade publishing companies, it's no wonder that unedited self-published books come out looking like poor second cousins.

You can put your book in the big leagues by treating your words with the same respect traditionally published authors treat theirs. Find a good editor.

If you go on-line to search for editing services, you will find thousands of choices. Some of those will be for stables of editors who work for companies that "outsource" the work, paying the editor a percentage of the fee they collect from the client. (The editor may get less than 50% of what you are charged, so many stables are full of low quality editors.) How do you sort through and find a good one?

1. Does the editor belong to professional organizations? There is no set standard for editors like there is for doctors or teachers. Anyone can call himself an editor. Those who

care about the profession band together to set standards for themselves. Find an editor who cares enough to join.

2. Does the editor offer a firm price based on your specific work? Editors can charge by the word, by the hour, or by the job. Beware an editor who offers to edit your book for a set fee without seeing your work. Editing is an art as well as a science and each piece of writing is unique. Be sure the editor sees the uniqueness of your project and its needs.

3. Does the editor offer a sample edit? This will give you and the editor a chance to see if you will work well together. Editing is a relationship and you both should feel happy that you are working together. The sample need not be long, but should offer the editor a good idea of what your needs as a writer are.

4. Does the editor offer an educative edit? This is specific to the needs of a self-publishing writer. In this type of editing, the editor works on a very short section of the writer's work and goes beyond fixing and moves to explaining why the changes are important. The writer goes back through the entire manuscript and uses the advice on the rest of the book. The writer actually becomes a better writer. Then the writer submits a second section of work. The process goes on until the writer and editor agree that the writer no longer needs that level of

support. (A writer should not need an educative edit on a whole book.) With an educative edit you gain a life skill that you can take into other writing projects.

5. Does the editor offer a guarantee? No one can turn a pig's ear into a silk purse, but the editor should be able to tell you what improvements you can expect.

6. Does the editor have satisfied clients willing to give references? Check them.
    When you have found the editor you want, agree on terms. You can do that through a signed agreement, or an agreement reached on-line.

7. It is common for editors to ask for at least half of the payment in advance. If the editor has given you a free sample edit, you can assume she will come through with the final edit as a professional. She has bought credibility with her free service and you can pay with confidence. If you have any difficulty with the editor and the editor belongs to a reputable association, use the association to resolve the dispute.

8. When you have a good editor who loves your work almost as much as you do, you stand head and shoulders above your fellow POD authors and your writing and marketing efforts will reap all the rewards you expect.

permission to copy or use this information, contact editor@writershelper.com

Audrey Owen, a writer who is both self-published and published by others in print and on-line, is an editor who specializes in working with self-publishing authors. Her Web site, http://www.writershelper.com, provides free writing tips and other information of interest to self-publishing authors.

Audrey Owen (Editors' Association of Canada, Federation of BC Writers—former regional director, Society of Children's Book Writers and Illustrators)
Editor for Self Publishers
494 Eaglecrest Drive
Gibsons, BC
CANADA
V0N 1V8

Approaching Agents & Publishers while Self-Publishing

By Dan Poynter

Many nonfiction book writers ask how to approach an agent or publisher. Today the question is when to approach them. Traditionally, writers had to decide between selling out and self-publishing. Their considerations were Often reduced to money, time and control.

Money. If your publisher prints 5000 copies, the book sells for $19.95 and your royalty is 6% of the cover price (12-14% of the net), your earnings will be less than $6000. If the book sells and goes back to press, you may do well.
Otherwise, it is not worth the many hours at the keyboard for $6000. According to Publishing for Profit by Tom Woll, most initial print runs are 5,000 copies.

In self-publishing, you invest the money but you do not have to share the net. You get it all.

The Publisher is the person or company that invests in the book.

Speed. It takes a large publisher 18 months to move a book through its system of production and distribution. From the time you deliver the manuscript, it will take a year and a half before books are on the shelves in the stores.

You can have a book printed in 2-5 weeks. You must consider: Do you want to wait an eternity to get paid? Will your information expire in 18 months? Will someone else beat you to the market with the same information? Do you want to let a publisher delay the publication of your book?

18 months? You can make a baby faster than that!

Control. Some of the larger publishers have surrendered to their bean counters. Many of their books are on pulp paper, the margins are narrow and the type is small. Your publisher may leave out some of your illustrations to save money.

As the (self) publisher, you can design the book to convey your information to your reader in the best-possible way.

A poorly produced book lacks credibility.
People won't buy the book and will never be exposed to the message.

Covering your bases. Today, with the computer and digital printing, it is possible to approach publishers and publish yourself. You can print 500 copies very reasonably (144 pages, 5.25 x 8.25, soft cover for $1,500). Then you can send the (example) book to agents and publishers.

Those who circulate a proposal, query letter or manuscript are treated like a writer.

Those with a book are treated like an author.

You will also send copies of your book to magazines for review, to book clubs for adoption and to foreign publishers for translation and publication.

Self-Published Books that were "Discovered" by Publishers

- *In Search of Excellence* by Tom Peters. Over 25,000 copies were sold directly to consumers in its first year. Then it was sold to Warner and the publisher sold 10 million more.

- *The Celestine Prophecy* by James Redfield. His manuscript made the rounds of the mainstream houses and then he decided to publish himself. He started by selling copies out of the trunk of his Honda—over 100,000 of them. He subsequently sold out to Warner Books for $800,000. Over 5.5 million copies have been sold.

- *The One-Minute Manager* by Ken Blanchard and Spencer Johnson sold over 20,000 copies locally before they sold out to William Morrow. It has now sold over 12-million copies since 1982 and is in 25 languages.

- *The Joy of Cooking* by Irma Rombauer was self-published in 1931 as a project of the First Unitarian Women's Alliance in

St. Louis. Today Scribners sells more than 100,000 copies each year.

- *What Color is Your Parachute* by Episcopal clergymen Richard Nelson Bolles. It is now published by Ten Speed Press.

- *Leadership Secrets of Attila the Hun* by Wess Roberts sold 486,000 copies before selling out to Warner Books.

Self-Publisher Overcame Rejection

He was a 34-year old advertising executive in Salt Lake City. He had two daughters, age six and four. He loved them very much—he told them so every day. But he wanted to express his love more permanently.
So, every night after he and his wife put the two girls to bed, he sat in the kitchen and wrote. After six week, he had completed 87 pages. He took them to a copy shop and reproduced 20 copies for family and friends.

They read his work and passed it on. After three weeks, 160 people had read his work. He was even contacted by a bookstore—they had customers asking for the "book".

Encouraged, he approached some publishers—and, of course, he was turned down. Not to be discouraged, he scraped together $5,000 and printed 9,000 copies. Then 19,000 more.

By the end of the year, he had sold over 250,000 copies.

And then, the publishers came looking for him! Simon & Schuster offered him $4.2 million—and he took it.

That was Richard Paul Evans and the book was The Christmas Box. It hit the top of the Publishers Weekly bestseller list and was translated into 13 Languages.

I teased him with "Rick, you were doing so well self-publishing and you sold out. Well, we all have our price. Your price is $4.2 million. (I suspect my price is a bit lower)."

Authors and promotion. Some authors do not want to publicly flog their books. You may be looking forward to the day when your work is recognized and you won't have to promote it. You may wish to be a celebrity and above all this crass commercialism. Be advised that Frank McCourt (Angela's Ashes) spends some six months each year making appearances on behalf of his books. He is a best-selling author because he promotes his books.

Whether you sell out to a (NY) publisher or publish yourself, the author must do the promotion. Publishers do not promote books. They have the books manufactured and they place them in bookstores. It is up to you to let potential buyers know your book is available.

There are four stages in the life of a book: writing, publishing, distributing and promoting. Giving birth to a book is like bringing a child into the world—you have an obligation to raise it. Fortunately, the book is not a twenty-year commitment and you do not have to send it to college. But, you do have to promote it.

You will write and promote your book and your publisher will produce and distribute it. You can deal with typesetters, printers and distributors yourself to get your finished book into the stores. You might as well self-publish.

Publishing increases the value. No one can be an expert in every book—some 100,000 titles are published each year. Everyone specializes or, at least, has a track record with certain categories of books. If you are turned down by an agent or publisher, that is not a reflection on the ability of the writer or the quality of the work. That agent or publisher just does not get it. With this New Model, if industry people fail to recognize the need and market for your book, it does not matter because your book is launched. It is out for review, it is to be considered by book clubs and evaluated foreign publishers. If an agent or publisher "discovers" your book after you have proven it in the market, it is now worth more. For examples, see the sidebars.

This New Book Model is the best approach for you, your book and
your writing future. Send your finished book to agents and publishers. Do not send a proposal, query letter or manuscript. Don't let the agents and publishers hold you back.

Writing periodicals:

Dan Poynter does not want you to die with a book still inside you. You have the ingredients and he has your recipe. Dan has written more than 100 books since 1969 including Writing Nonfiction and The Self-Publishing Manual. For more help on book writing, see http://ParaPub.com.
© 2003

or

Book Publishing periodicals:

Dan Poynter, the Voice of Self-Publishing, has written more than 100 books since 1969 including Writing Nonfiction and The Self-Publishing Manual. Dan is a past vice-president of the Publishers Marketing Association. For more help on book publishing and promoting, see http://ParaPub.com.
© 2003

or

Professional Speaking periodicals:

Dan Poynter has written more than 100 books since 1969 including Writing Nonfiction and The Self-Publishing Manual. He is past-chair of NSA's Writer- Publisher PEG and the founder of the PEG newsletter. For more help on book writing, publishing and promoting, see http://ParaPublishing.com.
© 2003

Publishing Tips and Specifications

Will Lulu lay out or edit my book for me?

No, Lulu provides you with the tools to publish and sell your books online, but it is up to you to do all the formatting and layout of your manuscript before you publish it on Lulu. That said, Lulu does have several ways for you to find formatting and editing help if you are uncomfortable doing it yourself.

Clicking the Services tab will take you to the, The Lulu Services Marketplace provides a place for authors and creators to connect with third-party service providers. These service providers, although handpicked by Lulu, *are not members of the Lulu staff.* The Services Marketplace simply brings together those seeking publishing services with those who provide them and handles financial transactions.

The Services Marketplace gives creators access to four broad categories of publishing services:

- **Editing services,** including manuscript reviews, proofreading and editing.
- **Graphics services,** including book cover design, illustrations and more.
- **Publishing services,** including manuscript formatting, PDF creation and consultation services.
- **Marketing services,** including press releases, websites and other marketing packages.

You can purchase services just like products on the site by clicking the "Add to Cart" button from the Service Details page. The Service Provider will contact you within 3 business days of your purchase to get started.

Make sure you carefully read through the complete description of a service before purchasing it. If you have questions about a specific service, contact that Service Provider directly via the "E-mail this provider" link on the service listing.

You can also peruse the, Lulu Support Forums. Lulu's expert users can provide you with many tips and tricks for preparing your manuscript for publishing on Lulu. Please be sure to search all of the help documentation for the answers to your questions before posting to the forums.

What types of files can I upload?

Lulu sends each book to its printer as a PDF (Portable Document Format). Lulu also distributes ebooks as PDF. You may either upload your book as a PDF or upload your manuscript in another format and have Lulu convert it to a PDF.

Adobe's Portable Document Format (PDF) is like a picture of your document. PDF files preserve the look and integrity of your original documents; they allow you the greatest control over the final appearance of your book, whether printed or distributed via download. PDFs are platform independent, which means they look and behave the same, regardless of hardware and software platforms on which they're displayed.

Mac, Windows, and Linux users will all see your document the way you intended!

If, like most authors, you want total control over how your book is going to look, convert your manuscript to PDF before uploading it. This will make for a bit more work on your part but will result in a published version of your book that looks exactly as you intended.

IMPORTANT: Lulu does not accept locked PDF files (those with edit or print access restricted). This is because our printers need full access to your file in order to print it correctly. Your unlocked PDF is secure: it is not available online.
If you have your document formatted as you want it but cannot generate PDFs, upload a file and have Lulu convert it to a PDF for you. We accept many file formats; they are listed below. If you upload a document that is not a PDF, the Lulu converter opens your document and generates a PDF.
You can upload a file in any of these formats to be converted to PDF:
- Microsoft Word
- Postscript
- Rich Text Format
- Microsoft Excel
- Microsoft PowerPoint
- Microsoft Works
- WordPerfect
- CGM (Computer Graphics Metafile)
- G3Fax (G3 Facsimile Image)
- GIF (Graphics Interchange Format)

- IEF (Image Exchange Format)
- JPEG (Joint Photographic Expert Group)
- PNG (Portable Network Graphic)
- NAPLPS (North American Presentation Layer Protocol)
- BTF (Personal Tree Bank Image Tiff)
- TIFF (Tagged Image File Format)
- AutoCAD Drawing
- FPX (Flash Pix Format)
- SVF (Simple Vector Format)
- BMP (Windows Bitmap)
- XIFF (Extended Image File Format)
- CMU Raster (Carnegie-Mellon Raster)
- Portable Anymap
- Portable Bitmap
- Portable Graymap
- Portable Pixmap
- Bitmap
- Raw RGB image (Red-green-blue image)
- X Bitmap
- X Pixmap
- SGML (Standard Generalized Markup Language)
- XML (Extensible Markup Language)

If you plan to upload your document for conversion to PDF, embed any separate images in your document before uploading. That is, save them with the document file. Do not include or link to them by reference.

The Lulu PDF generator and conversion process accepts the following image formats:

- Enhanced Metafile (EMF)
- Windows Metafile (WMF)
- JPEG File Interchange Format (JPG, JPEG, JFIF, JPE)
- Portable Network Graphics (PNG)
- Windows Bitmap (BMP, DBC, RLE, BMZ)
- Graphics Interchange Format (GIF, GFA)

How big should my margins be?

Leave at least .5" margins on all your pages. Most books will require a gutter of .2" to .3". A *gutter* provides a little bit of extra margin on the spine edge of your pages, making your book easier to read without putting too much stress on the spine. For coil-bound books, the coils bite about 5/16" (8mm) on the spine edge, but we would suggest a gutter of 3/8" (9mm). Follow these directions to set your margins:

- **Microsoft Word:** Choose Page Setup from the File menu, then use the Margins tab. When adding a gutter, make sure to select Mirror Margins. Apply your settings to the whole document.
- **Microsoft Works:** Choose Page Setup from the File menu, then use the Margins tab. Works has no provision for a gutter.
- **Open Office:** Choose Page from the Format menu. To create a gutter, add the desired gutter to the inside

margin dimension. Then select Mirrored under the Layout Settings, Page Layout choices

When creating your book, make sure that your title page falls on an odd-numbered page (on the right-hand side of your book) and the copyright page falls on an even-numbered page (on the left-hand side of your book).

What fonts can I use in my document?

If you are planning to upload your own PDF, you may use any fonts you like, but you must embed the fonts in the PDF before uploading to Lulu. If you are planning to have Lulu convert your document to a PDF, be sure to choose fonts from the following list. If you use a font that is not on this list, the Lulu converter will substitute one of these fonts in its place. This may adversely affect your formatting.

- Arial
- Book Antigua
- Bookman Old Style
- Century
- Courier
- Garamond
- Palatino
- Tahoma
- Times New Roman
- Verdana

- Symbols

Follow these general guidelines when choosing your fonts:
- Serif fonts are best for printed documents. Use serif fonts like Garamond, Times New Roman and Palatino for blocks of body text.
- Sans serif fonts are best for online documents and for display text. Use sans serif fonts like Arial and Verdana if you intend your book to be viewed online.
- Use bold sans serif fonts for title text or headings.

How to Create a PDF File

We highly recommend using Adobe Acrobat to convert your book to a PDF. (If you plan to purchase the Global Distribution Service, your PDF *must* be distilled by Adobe.) Acrobat can be purchased from Adobe (http://www.adobe.com) or any software retailer.

If you do not want to buy the software, try these options:
- Adobe offers an online subscription service that allows you to pay a fee to turn a set number documents into PDF files (http://createpdf.adobe.com).
- CutePDF (http://www.cutepdf.com/) is a free PDF-creation program
- PDF Creator is installed as a printer driver. To create a PDF, open your document, then print to the PDF Creator "printer." The result is a PDF file.

Before you install PDF Creator, you need to install a PostScript Print Driver that has custom page sizes. I use HP LaserJet 5/5m Postscript. Install your Postscript Driver, set it as the default printer and go to paper and setup a custom page size. Then install PDF Creator and set it as the default printer with your custom page size. Reboot your system and go to printer setting to make sure that your custom page size held. Next open your document, go to file, top left side of Microsoft Word and select print. Make sure the printer selected is PDF Creator, then place a check in the print to file box and click on the OK button. This will create a .PRN file. I then go to Adobe Online (http://createpdf.adobe.com/) to create my PDF file, just to make sure that I have an Adobe signature on my file. You can subscribe to Create Adobe PDF Online for $9.99 a month or you can take advantage of their free trial offer that allows you to create 5 free PDF files, if the file isn't too large. I had no problem creating this book with the free trial offer. I usually select the Web default setting and Acrobat 4.0 compatibility with no security settings.

If you are planning to create a PDF using Apple's Pages software, you should know that this software often creates sub-optimal PDFs and can cause problems when printing, especially with commercial printers like Lulu's. The most often cited problem with these PDFs is multiple embedded subsets of fonts. For a workaround to this problem, read the tutorial at http://www.anvilwerks.com/pages_workaround/.
This workaround is not a universal fix.

How can I be sure my PDF will print correctly?

If you are uploading your own PDF, follow these guidelines.

For paperbacks

Settings for exporting to PDF or creating from Distiller:

- Fully embed all fonts used in the document. Subsetted fonts over multiple pages can cause problems when your PDF is rasterized for print. Your document may be printed with symbols instead of fonts, garbled text or missing text.
- Set compatibility mode to Acrobat 5
- Leave the PDF's colorspace in its original profile. Do not convert CMYK to RGB or vice versa.
- Turn off Overprint and Simulate Overprint
- The PDF filesize should not exceed 700MB
- Do not downsample your images unless they are fully rasterized. If they are fully rasterized and the DPI is greater than 300, downsample to 300 DPI.
- Flatten your final PDF to a single layer.

Settings for image files within the PDF:

- Image compression should be set to ZIP if you want lossless (no artifacts/distortion-free) images. To reduce filesize, use JPEG -> High.
- If you are printing a color book that has black & white images in it, the black & white images should have the colorspace set to grayscale.
- Leave the images' colorspace in their original profiles. Do not convert CMYK to RGB or vice versa.
- Do not use CCITT or LZW compression. LZW compression creates multi-strip images, which may show white lines when printed.
- Use ZIP encoding for grayscale images.
- The gamma of a grayscale image should be between 2.2 and 2.4.
- DPI should be between 300 and 600 DPI.

How do I change the size of my PDF in Adobe Distiller?

If you are using Adobe Acrobat Distiller, the default page setting is 8.5" x 11". To create a PDF of another size, you must change the PDF settings in Acrobat Distiller by following these instructions:

1. Open Acrobat Distiller.
2. From the Settings menu, select Edit Adobe PDF Settings. The General settings are displayed.
3. In the Default Page Size fields, enter the desired width and height of your document.

4. Click Save As and enter a descriptive name for the job options file.

Our print-on-demand process currently supports only black and white *or* color printing. If your document is a black and white book, make sure the print settings on Acrobat Distiller are set for black and white.

How do I embed fonts in a PDF?

If you are planning to upload your own PDF, you may use any fonts you like, but you must embed the fonts in the PDF before uploading to Lulu. If you are using Acrobat Distiller to create your PDF file, edit the job options to embed your fonts.

1. Open Acrobat Distiller.
2. From the Settings menu, select Edit Adobe PDF Settings. The General settings are displayed.
3. Click the Fonts folder and select Embed All Fonts.

If you are using the CreatePDF service from Adobe (http://createpdf.adobe.com):

1. Click Preferences.
2. Under Document Options, select Press or Print from the dropdown menu in the Optimization Settings field.
3. Click the edit settings link next to the Optimization Settings field and ensure that Embed All Fonts and Subset Embedded Fonts are checked

How do I insert images into my document?

There are many ways to insert images into your documents. An easy way to ensure that your image stays where you want it is to create a paragraph in your word processing document to hold the image, then insert it. To insert an image in a Microsoft Word document:

1. Move the insertion point to the end of the paragraph that introduces your image. Press Enter.
2. With the insertion point in the new paragraph, select Picture > From File from the Insert menu. (You can also paste an image from the clipboard.)
3. Browse to select the file, then click Insert.
4. Adjust the sizing and placement of the image:
   - Resize the image so that it fits in the text boundaries.
   - Use the cropping tools to remove extra white space from the image.
   - Select Paragraph from the Format menu and change spacing above and below to add padding around the image.
   - Use paragraph alignment to center- or left-align the image.
   - Select Reference > Caption from the Insert menu to add a figure caption to the image.
5. Save your document.

Full Bleed Interior Pages

How do I make my content stretch all the way to the edge of the page (full bleed)?

1. Upload your book as a single PDF. (It has to be one PDF or it will not bypass the converter. The converters

size content to the exact cutting dimension, so there will often be a thin sliver of white if you upload a document that needs conversion.)

2. Make the leading edge bleed .25" (75 pixels at 300dpi). The leading edge is the outside edge — non-bound or loose.
3. Make the top and bottom bleeds .125" (37 or 38 pixels at 300dpi). Total combined bleed for top and bottom edges will be .25" (75 pixels at 300dpi).

NOTE: Bear in mind that anything within the bleed area is likely to be cut off, so don't have any critical text or artwork within a half inch (.5") of the edges. Use this chart to figure out dimensions for your final PDF document.

When you publish a full bleed PDF, the size that shows up on the site will round up, so a 6x9 book using a 6.25" x 9.25" source PDF will show as 6.3" x 9.3". Don't worry about this; it will print as 6x9 and trim the bleeds correctly.

Final PDF Dimensions for Full Bleed (interior)

Book Size,	Size of PDF to Upload,	Size in Pixels
6" x 9",	6.25" x 9.25"	1875 x 2775
8.5" x 11",	8.75" x 11.25"	2625 x 3375
8.25" x 10.75	8.5" x 11.0"	2550 x 1100
Comic, 6.625" x 10.25",	6.875" x 10.5",	2062 x 3150
Landscape, 9" x 7",	9.25" x 7.25",	2775 x 2175
Square, 7.5" x 7.5",	7.75" x 7.75",	2325 x 2325
Pocket Size, 4.25" x 6.875",	4.5" x 7.125",	1350 x 2138

Crown Quarto, 18.9cm x 24.6cm ,19.27cm x 25.24cm, 2307 x 2979
A4, 21.0cm x 29.7cm 21.64cm x 30.34cm 2556 x 3582

The pixels are basically three times your inches to derive 300 DPI. You can set your page at 300 DPI and then scale it back to about 25% to work with.

What resolution (DPI) should my images have to achieve optimum print quality?

We've tested print quality at various resolutions and found that 300dpi is the optimum resolution. 600dpi is our limit at this time, but any improvement in print quality over 300dpi is not noticeable, and the file size is huge.

Should I use CMYK, RGB or grayscale images?

Depending on which type of binding you choose for your book, there are different ways to optimize your document for print.

- **For all black & white books (except comic size)**, the source document and images should be in RGB mode.
- **For full color books**, the source document and/or images should be in the original colorspace. If it was created in RGB, DO NOT convert it to CMYK and vice versa.
  - **If your full color book contains black & white images**, set each black & white image to grayscale.

How can I make sure my images will print exactly as I want them to?

When you include illustrations, photographs and other images in your book, most times they will print correctly. There are a few things you can do to ensure the picture quality is what you expect.

- If you are uploading images inside your own PDF, see How can I be sure my PDF will print correctly?
- Before uploading, print your source document and review how the images print.
- If you are uploading a PDF, print the PDF and review how the images translated into the PDF.
- After Lulu converts your file, you must view and approve the conversion. Click View, then use your browser's print function to print a review copy.

Should I include my cover in the same file as the rest of my book?

No, your cover should be completely separate from your main document. You will upload your cover file(s) in a separate step of the publishing process.

What types of files can I upload for my book cover?

You have two options for uploading your book cover. You may upload separate front and back covers, or you may upload a single one-piece (wrap-around) cover. Cover files that are uploaded separately must be JPG, GIF or PNG files of at least

300dpi. One-piece (wrap-around) cover files must be PDF. You may not use a Word document as your cover.

Tips for creating your one-piece cover PDF

Since we have introduced one-piece covers, we have seen a number of covers that have trouble printing. This is because our automated cover creation process created a PDF that was flattened to a single layer. However, it is possible to create a very complex PDF using Adobe Illustrator with many layers, fonts etc. *Don't do this.*

The more complex the PDF, the greater chance that the process of rasterizing for print will generate errors. If you've created a cover PDF that uses fonts and separate images, your best option is to open the PDF in PhotoShop — it will automatically ask for DPI (300 is optimal) and color palette (choose RGB). It will then rasterize the file to a single layer.

What programs can I use to create my book cover?

Book covers can be made using several different design programs. We recommend Adobe PhotoShop, Adobe Illustrator, and PaintShop Pro. However, there are other programs that will work just as well. If you have one of these programs, you should either know how to use it already or learn from a friend how to use it before attempting to make your own cover.

Will Lulu design and/or create my book cover for me?

No, Lulu provides you with the tools to publish and sell your books online, but it is up to you to do all the formatting and design of your book before you publish it on Lulu. That said, Lulu does have several ways for you to find cover creation help if you are uncomfortable doing it yourself.

During the publishing process, Lulu offers a gallery of free covers for you to use. These covers won't necessarily be as personalized as you might like, but they look great. The Lulu cover wizard will insert your title and author name on the front cover automatically and will put your ISBN bar code (if you purchased one) on the back cover.

Clicking the SERVICES tab will take you to the Lulu Services Marketplace. The Lulu Services Marketplace provides a place for authors and creators to connect with third-party service providers. These service providers, although handpicked by Lulu, *are not members of the Lulu staff*. The Services Marketplace simply brings together those seeking publishing services with those who provide them and handles financial transactions.

The Services Marketplace gives creators access to four broad categories of publishing services:

- **Graphics services**, including book cover design, illustrations and more.
- **Editing services**, including manuscript reviews, proofreading and editing.
- **Publishing services**, including manuscript formatting, PDF creation and consultation services.

- **Marketing services,** including press releases, websites and other marketing packages.

You can purchase services just like products on the site by clicking the "Add to Cart" button from the Service Details page. The Service Provider will contact you within 3 business days of your purchase to get started.

Make sure you carefully read through the complete description of a service before purchasing it. If you have questions about a specific service, contact that Service Provider directly via the "E-mail this provider" link on the service listing.

You can also peruse the Lulu Support Forums. Lulu's expert users can provide you with many tips and tricks for creating your book cover. Please be sure to search all of the help documentation for the answers to your questions before posting to the forums.

What is the difference between a one-piece cover and separate front and back covers?

One-piece covers allow for complete customization of your book cover. Uploading a one-piece cover is the only way to create a design on the spine of your book. (Standard spines must be a solid color. You may opt to have the book's title printed on the spine.)

Lulu will not add anything to your one-piece cover, including an ISBN bar code. If you plan to upload a one-piece cover for your ISBN book, you must generate your own bar code and add it to your cover.

One-piece (wrap around) cover files must be PDF. Cover files that are uploaded separately must be JPG, GIF or PNG files of at least 300dpi.

What dimensions should my book cover have?

Front and back cover images should be the same size. It is important that the image files you upload for your cover are larger than the book's size, because the edges will be trimmed off or folded over during production. The area that will be trimmed is known as *bleed*. The bleed area is on the perimeter of the cover and should be filled with the background image or color, but remain free of any text and/or images that should not be cut off. The perimeter of casewrap hardcovers should also be filled with the background image or color because they will be folded over when the book is constructed.

The bleed for all books (those sold through Lulu and through distribution services) is .375" (1 cm). Use this chart to determine what size your book cover image files should be.

You might notice that the cover dimensions for hardcover books are slightly larger than the size of the text block. This is normal; most hardcovers extend beyond the edges of the interior pages

Size of Book Cover Image to Upload, Size in Pixels

Paperback Books,   image size & pixels (book covers)

6" x 9"	6.375" x 9.75"	1913 x 2925
8.5" x 11"	8.875" x 11.75"	2663 x 3525
Comic, 6.625" x 10.25"	7" x 11"	2100 x 3300
Landscape, 9" x 7"	9.375" x 7.75"	2813 x 2325
Square, 7.5" x 7.5"	7.875" x 8.25"	2363 x 2475
Pocket 4.25" x 6.875"	4.625" x 7.625"	1388 x 2288

International Paperbacks (book covers)

Royal, 15.6cm x 23.4cm	17.6cm x 24.4cm	2077 x 2879
Crown Quarto, 18.9cm x 24.6cm	19.9cm x 26.6cm	2345 x 3129
A4, 21.0cm x 29.7cm	22.0cm x 31.7cm	2594 x 3732

Hardcover Books (book covers)

6" x 9"	6.5" x 10"	1950 x 3000
8.25" x 10.75"	8.75" x 11.75"	2625 x 3525

If you purchase the Global Distribution Service for your book, your book cover and text files are uploaded to and stored with a different vendor. Their requirements are stricter than the Lulu printer. **If you do not meet these requirements, the availability of your book to online retailers will be delayed for several days, possibly weeks!** Please make sure you meet all dimension requirements before you approve your book for Global Distribution. You will have to pay a fee to make changes.

What dimensions should my one-piece (wrap-around) cover have?

Your one-piece (wrap around) cover file must be a PDF. Unlike separate front and back covers, the one-piece cover uploader will not accept image files. The correct dimensions of your cover will be given during Step 4 of the publishing process. Please make sure you match these dimensions or your cover will not be accepted.

The table below shows the dimensions for one-piece covers for paperback books. If you have already prepared your manuscript and know its size and page count, you can use this spine size calculator to calculate the width of your spine, then add the spine width to the dimensions shown below to determine the dimensions of your one piece cover PDF.

Paperback books (one-piece book cover)

6" x 9" 12.25" (+ spine) x 9.25" 3675 (+ spine) x 2775
8.5" x 11" 17.25" (+ spine) x 11.25" 5175 (+ spine) x 3375
Comic, 6.625" x 10.25" 13.5" (+ spine) x 10.5" 4050 (+ spine) x 3150
Landscape, 9" x 7" 18.25" (+ spine) x 7.25" 5475 (+ spine) x 2175

Square, 7.5" x 7.5" 15.25" (+ spine) x 7.75" 4575 (+ spine) x 2325

Pocket Size, 4.25" x 6.875" 8.75" (+ spine) x 7.125" 2625 (+ spine) x 2138

International Paperbacks (one-piece book cover)

Royal, 15.6cm x 23.4cm 31.9cm (+ spine) x 24.1cm 3764 (+ spine) x 2844

Crown Quarto, 18.9cm x 24.6cm 38.5cm (+ spine) x 25.3cm 4539 (+ spine) x 2979

A4, 21.0cm x 29.7cm 42.7cm (+ spine) x 30.4cm 5037 (+ spine) x 3582

Hardcover books Dust Jacket (one-piece book cover)

6" x 9" 19.25" (+ spine) x 9.5" 5775 (+ spine) x 2850

Casewrap 6" x 9" 13.75" (+ spine) x 10.75" 4125 (+ spine) x 3225

Casewrap 8.25" x 10.75" 18.25" (+ spine) x 12.5" 5475 (+ spine) x 3750

Keep in mind that the cover dimensions for hardcover books are slightly larger than the size of the text block. This is normal; most hardcovers extend beyond the edges of the interior pages.

This is the equation for determining the dimensions of a one-piece cover for a dust jacket hardcover:

Bleed + Back Flap + Back Cover + Spine + Front Cover + Front Flap + Bleed

This is the equation for determining the dimensions of a one-piece cover for a casewrap hardcover:

Turn-in bleed + Back Cover + Spine + Front Cover + Turn-in Bleed

How much space should I leave on my back cover for my ISBN barcode?

If you plan to purchase a distribution service for your book or if you are planning to enter your own ISBN for your book, you will need to leave a **3.625" x 1.25"** area on the bottom right corner of your back cover that is free of any text and/or images that should not be cut off. This area is for your bar code, ISBN and Content ID number.

Your ISBN bar code will be automatically generated by Lulu if you are using separate front and back covers. If you upload a one-piece (wrap-around) cover, you are responsible for generating and including your ISBN bar code in your one-piece PDF. Lulu will not automatically generate ISBN bar codes for one-piece (wrap-around) covers.

If you are planning to purchase the Global Distribution Service for your book, Ingram requests that if you include your retail price on the book cover, it must exactly match your retail price that you set on Lulu. If it does not match, it will be removed. Likewise, we ask that you do not add an UK retail price to the cover, as this number will be converted by us and it most likely will not match what you come up with.

If you are planning to purchase the Global Distribution Service for your book, it is important to know that your book cover and text files will be uploaded to and stored with a different printer.

This printer's requirements are stricter than the Lulu printer. **If you do not meet these requirements, the availability of your book to online retailers will be delayed for several days, possibly weeks!** Please make sure you meet all dimension requirements before you approve your book for global distribution!

Will my ISBN barcode be automatically generated on my one-piece cover?

No, you must include your own bar code for your one-piece cover. Unlike separate front and back covers, your ISBN bar code will not be automatically added to your one-piece cover. It is up to you to add every element you would like to appear on your one-piece cover, as this type of cover allows for total customization.

Can I purchase a distribution service before uploading my file, so I can put the ISBN on my one-piece cover?

No, this is not possible at this time. You may only purchase distribution services for published books, because ISBNs must be assigned to specific content. If you plan to use a one-piece cover, you may follow these steps to include your ISBN on your cover:

1. Publish your book. (You can make it Available only to me if you are not ready to release it to the public.)

2. Purchase the Basic Distribution Service. An ISBN will be assigned to your book and will appear in your Project List next to the title.
3. Revise your cover to include the ISBN
4. Make your book Available to the public.
5. Upgrade to Global Distribution if you would like to do so.

Mandatory Requirements for Global Distribution

The industry requires that your book adheres to its distribution standards, and it is up to you to ensure your book meets the requirements. If your book is submitted to the industry before it meets these requirements, it will be rejected and your book distribution will be delayed while you work to bring your book into compliance. These are the requirements your book must meet prior to distribution:

Requirements for all book covers

- If you include your retail price on the cover, it must exactly match the retail price you set on your book. Lulu will not add the price to your book cover.
- Keep all text and images at least 0.375" from all sides of the cover. This area may be trimmed off. (This includes .25" bleed area and .125" safety area.) If you are uploading a one-piece cover, use these dimensions:

	(Width x Height)	(Size in Pixels)
6" x 9"	12.25" (+ spine) x 9.25"	3675 (+ spine) x 2775
8.5" x 11"	17.25" (+ spine) x 11.25"	5175 (+ spine) x 3375

Spine text must be at least .0625" away from all edges of the spine. Text that is too close to the edge of the spine will be reduced in size to fit. (This may result in very small text on the spine of your book.)

Additional requirements for one-piece covers

- Cover must have correct ISBN/EAN.
- Bar codes must be provided in black and white.
- Bar codes should be 1.833" wide by 1" high.

Requirements for book interiors

- The book description should be between 40 and 4,000 characters; longer descriptions may not be displayed by booksellers.
- Text must be an Adobe distilled PDF. (If you provide your own PDF it must be distilled using Adobe; if you upload a word processing document, Lulu will distill it using Adobe.)
- Embed all fonts (and all font family members used) when distilling your PDF.
- Perfect bound books: Should have no fewer than 80 pages and no more than 740 pages. (Books with less than 80 pages must include enough blank pages to reach a minimum of 80 pages or they will be saddle-stitched.)
- Saddle-stitched books: Should have between 48 and 76 pages. Anything over 76 will be padded up to 80 and will therefore be perfect bound.
- Total page count must be divisible by four. Blank pages will be added to achieve this if necessary.

- Final page of each book must be completely blank.
- Book must have a copyright page with your correct ISBN/EAN.
- Book must have a title page.
- Margins must be at least .5" on all sides. Your left margin must be equal to your right margin, and your top margin must be equal to your bottom margin.
- You may add a gutter to your document in addition to your margins.
- Page numbering must be correct. No page numbers may be skipped.
- Interior text and images should be submitted as grayscale only. NO CMYK or RGB files.
- All files should be submitted at high-resolution (300 dpi).

Books with the global distribution package will be printed and distributed from the US and the UK.

Library of Congress Control Number (LCCN)

A Library of Congress catalog card number is a unique identification number that the Library of Congress assigns to the catalog record created for each book in its cataloged collections. Librarians use it to locate a specific Library of Congress catalog record in the national databases and to order catalog cards from the Library of Congress or from commercial suppliers. The Library of Congress assigns this number while the book is being cataloged. Under certain circumstances, however, a card number can be assigned before the book is published through the Pre-assigned Card Number Program. http://pcn.loc.gov/

Publishers participating in the program complete a Pre-assigned Control Number Application form for each title for which a pre-assigned control number is requested. Based on the information provided by the publisher, Library staff pre-assigns a control number to each eligible title. Upon receiving the number, the publisher prints it on the back of the title page (i.e., the copyright page) in the following manner:

Library of Congress Control Number: 2004012345

The purpose of the Pre-assigned Control Number (PCN) program is to enable the Library of Congress to assign control numbers in advance of publication to those titles that may be added to the Library's collections. The publisher prints the control number in the book and thereby facilitates cataloging and other book processing activities. The PCN links the book to any record, which the Library of Congress, other libraries, bibliographic utilities, or book vendors may create.

Only U.S. book publishers are eligible to participate in the PCN program. These publishers must list a U.S. place of publication on the title page or copyright page of their books and maintain an editorial office in the U.S. capable of answering substantive bibliographic questions.

To obtain Library of Congress card numbers for your forthcoming books, you must first complete the Application to Participate and obtain an account number and password. The account number and password will provide you access to the appropriate form for requesting Library of Congress card numbers.

PCN policy is to provide only one account number for each participating publisher. Particularly large houses may warrant exception to this policy. Those houses should contact their Publisher Liaison for further guidance upon establishing their first account.

Please be sure to read the following before completing the Application to Participate:

- The purpose of the PCN program
- The PCN process
- Publisher eligibility
- Scope of the PCN program

Please also note that a JavaScript-enabled browser such as Netscape 4.5 or Microsoft Explorer 4.0 or higher is required to complete the application to participate and the subsequent form to request Library of Congress card numbers.

If, after reading the above, your house appears eligible to participate in the PCN program, please complete the Application to Participate.

Cite yourself or your company's name as the publisher. It's best to apply for your LCCN after you acquire your ISBN with the basic package. Once you have approved global distribution, you're officially published.

Happy Selling!

Index

G

H

I

J

K

L

S

T

U

W

Made in the USA